EASY PIANO

the music glee
season three volume seven

GW00776940

ISBN 978-1-4584-2345-0

7777 W. Bluemound Rd. P.O. Box 13819 Milwaukee, WI 53213

Visit Hal Leonard Online at
www.halleonard.com

YOU CAN'T STOP THE BEAT

from HAIRSPRAY

Music by MARC SHAIMAN
Lyrics by MARC SHAIMAN and SCOTT WITTMAN

1
1 2
1
- sons, girl, but you know you nev - er will. And you can
of time, but ya know it just can't be. And if they
and fork when I see a Christ - mas ham. So if you

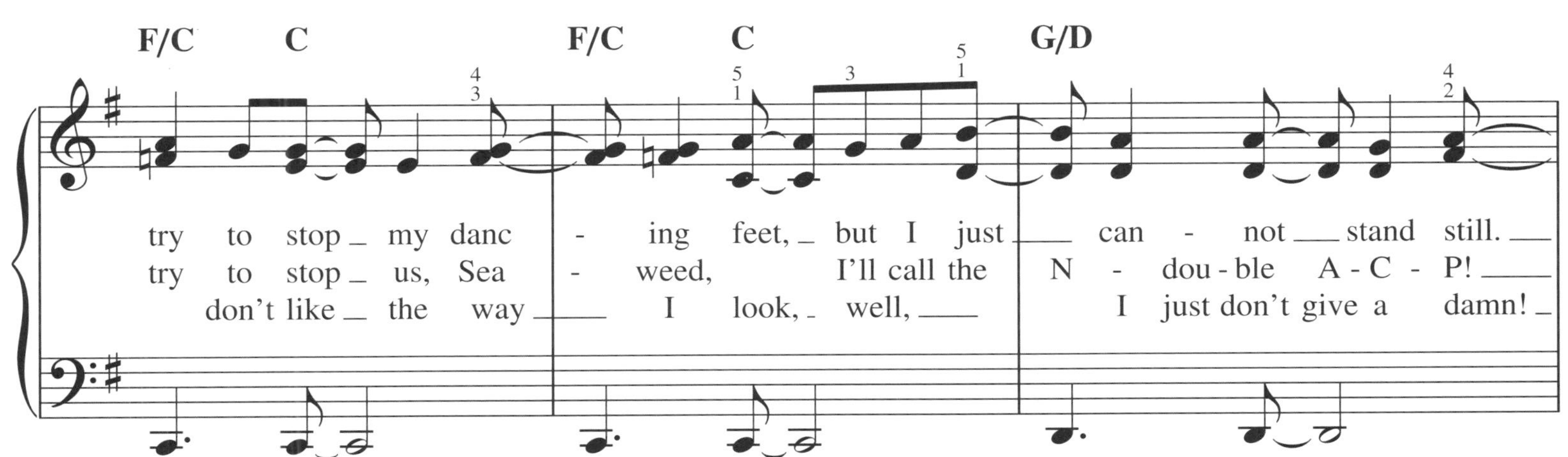
F/C C F/C C G/D
try to stop my danc - ing feet, but I just can - not stand still.
try to stop us, Sea - weed, I'll call the N - dou - ble A - C - P!
don't like the way I look, well, I just don't give a damn!

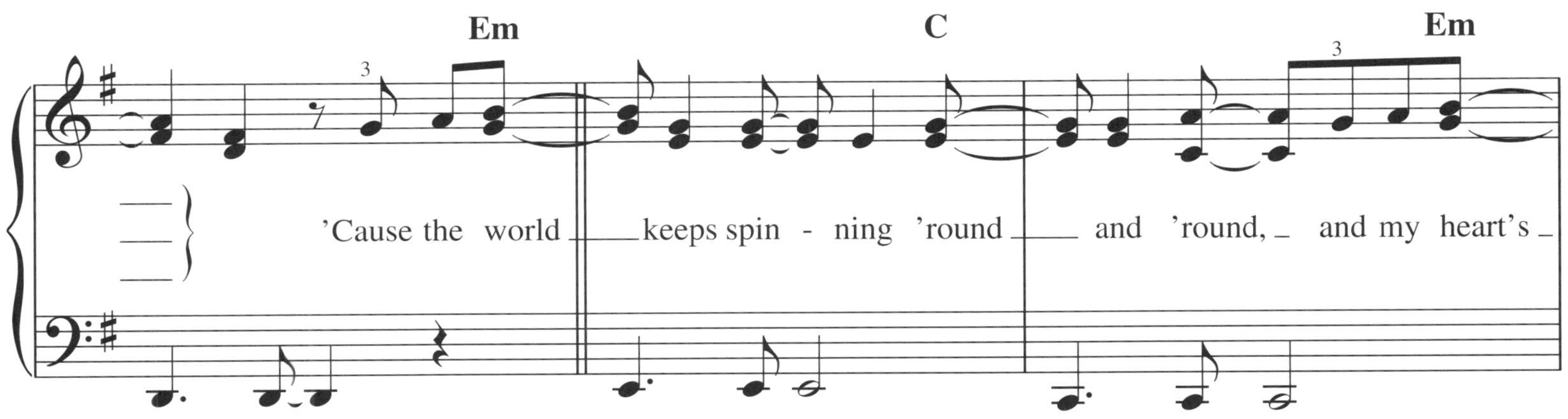
Em C Em
'Cause the world keeps spin - ning 'round and 'round, and my heart's

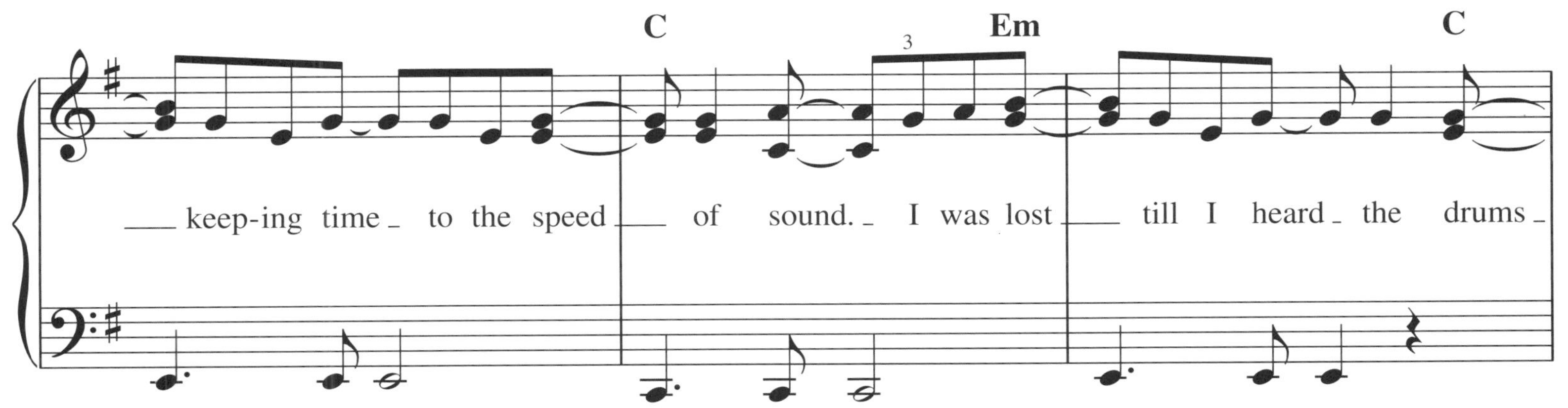
C Em C
keep-ing time to the speed of sound. I was lost till I heard the drums

D
D7 G/D D Dsus
then I found my way
'cause you can't stop the beat!

G C G C G C
(1.,3.) Ev - er since this old world be - gan a wom - an found out if she shook it, she could
(2.,4.) Ev - er since we first saw the light, a man and wom - an like to shake it on a

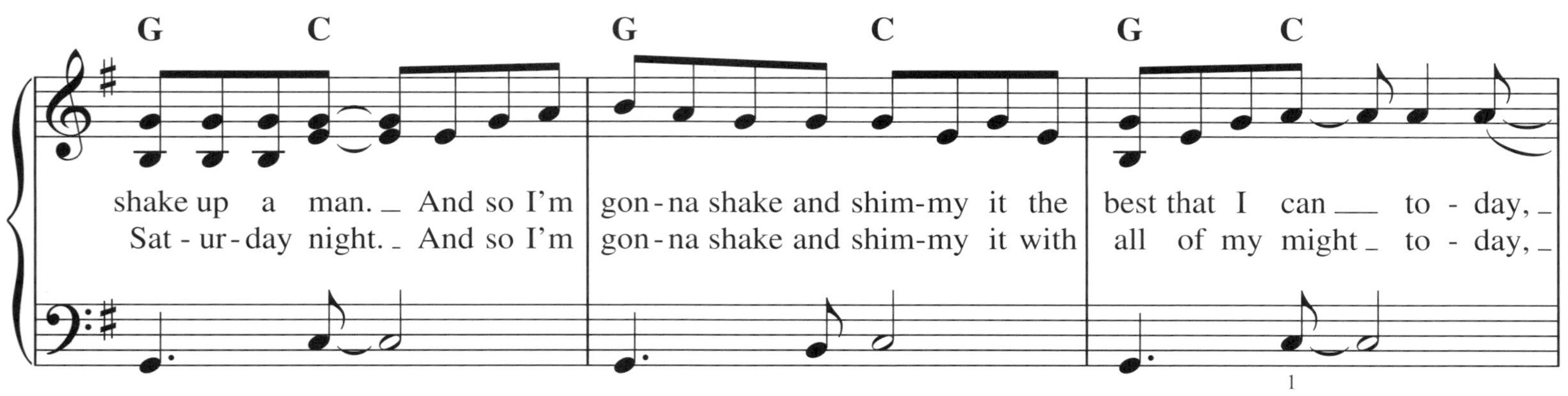
G C G C G C
shake up a man. And so I'm gon - na shake and shim - my it the best that I can to - day,
Sat - ur - day night. And so I'm gon - na shake and shim - my it with all of my might to - day,

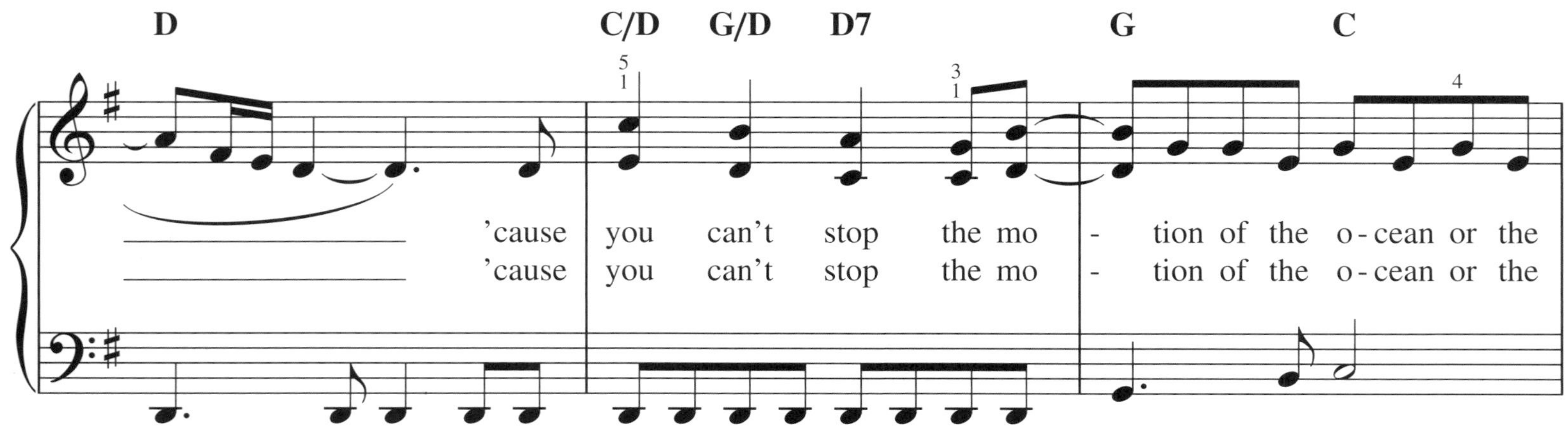
D C/D G/D D7 G C
'cause you can't stop the mo - tion of the o - cean or the
'cause you can't stop the mo - tion of the o - cean or the

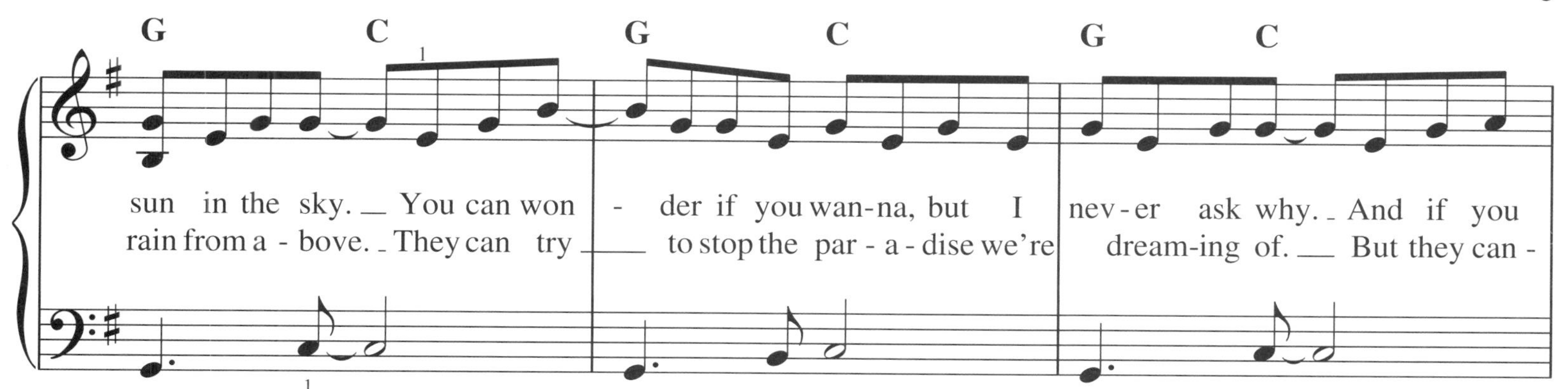
G C G C G C
sun in the sky. You can won - der if you wan-na, but I nev-er ask why. And if you
rain from a - bove. They can try to stop the par - a - dise we're dream-ing of. But they can -

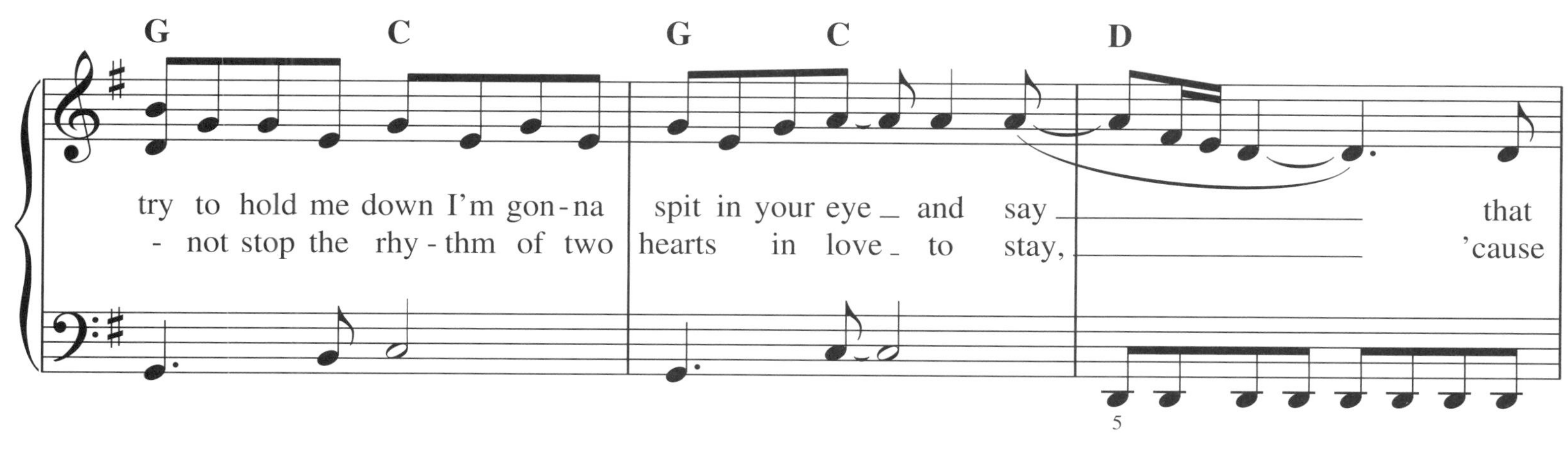
G C G C D
try to hold me down I'm gon-na spit in your eye and say that
- not stop the rhy - thm of two hearts in love to stay, 'cause

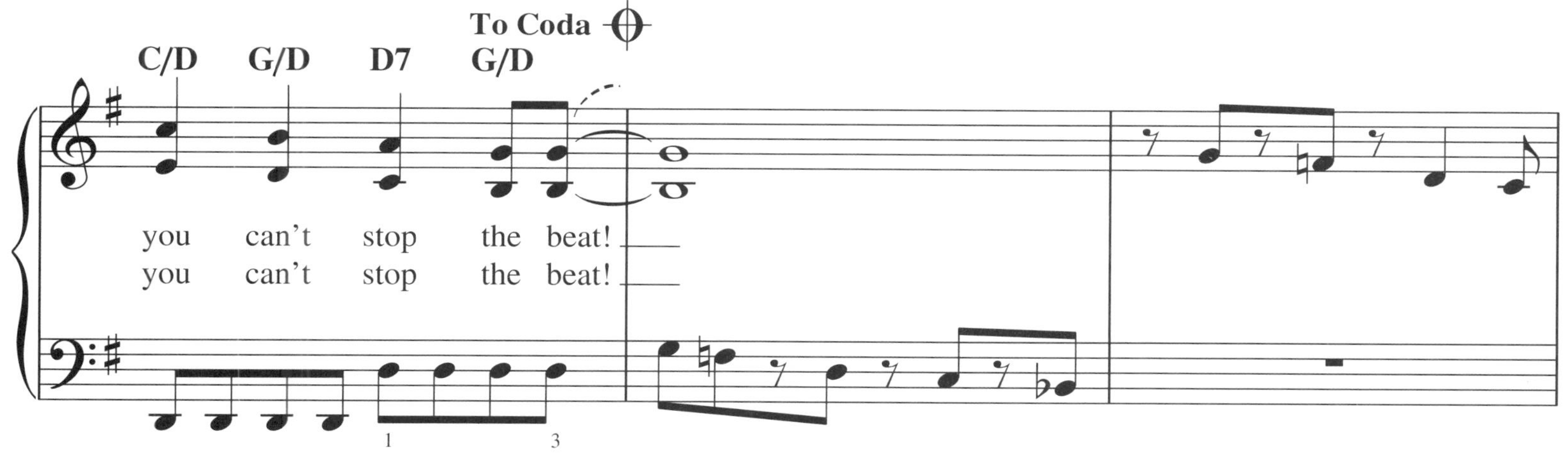
To Coda
C/D G/D D7 G/D
you can't stop the beat!
you can't stop the beat!

1., 2.
F♯7
3.
D.C. al Coda
F♯7

CODA
E7
Ah,
ah, ah.
Ah,

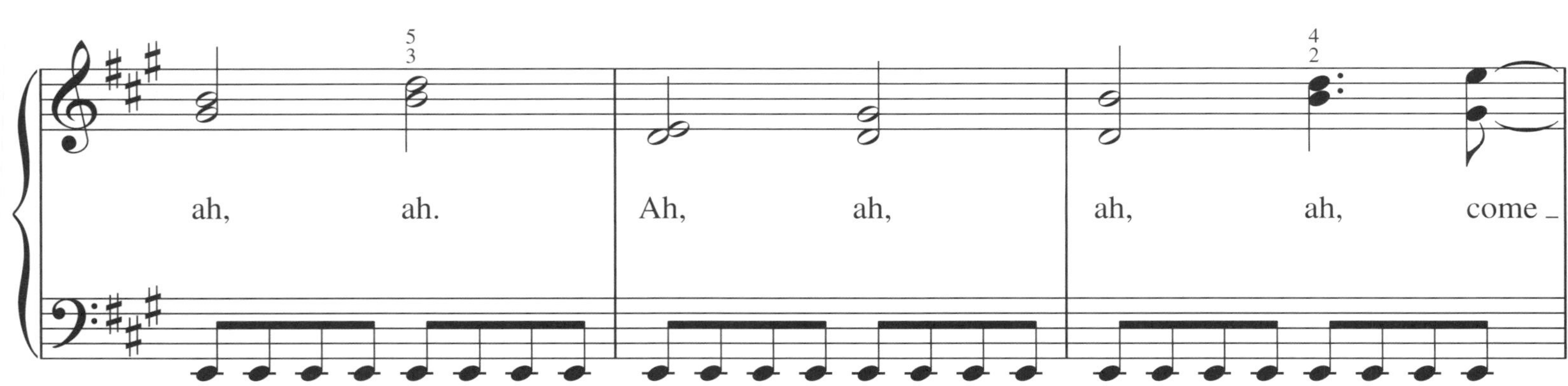
5
3
4
2
ah, ah.
Ah, ah,
ah, ah, come

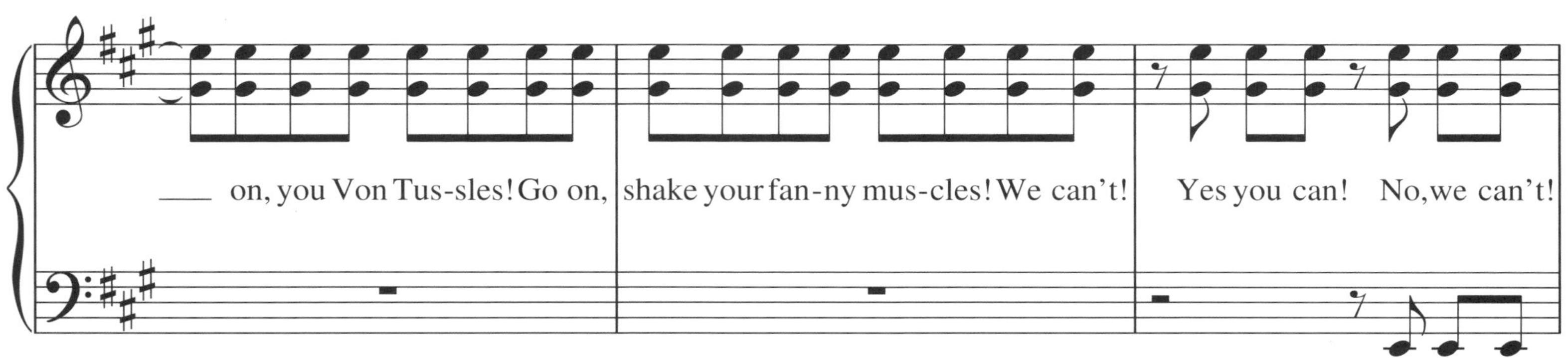
on, you Von Tus-sles! Go on,
shake your fan-ny mus-cles! We can't!
Yes you can! No, we can't!

4
2
Yes, you can! Yes, we can!
You can't stop the beat!

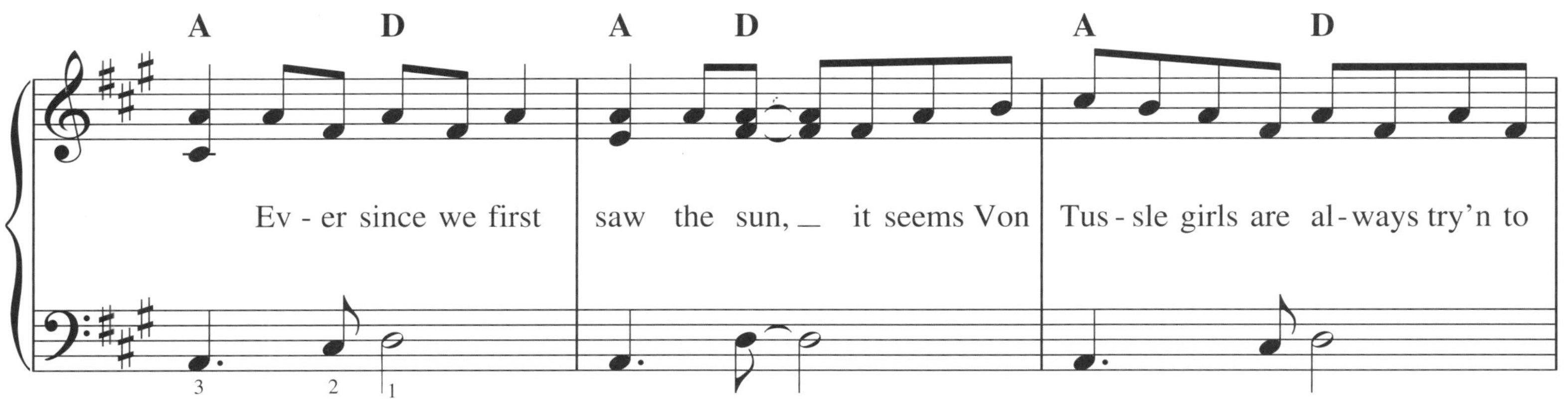
A D A D A D
Ev - er since we first saw the sun, it seems Von Tus - sle girls are al - ways try'n to

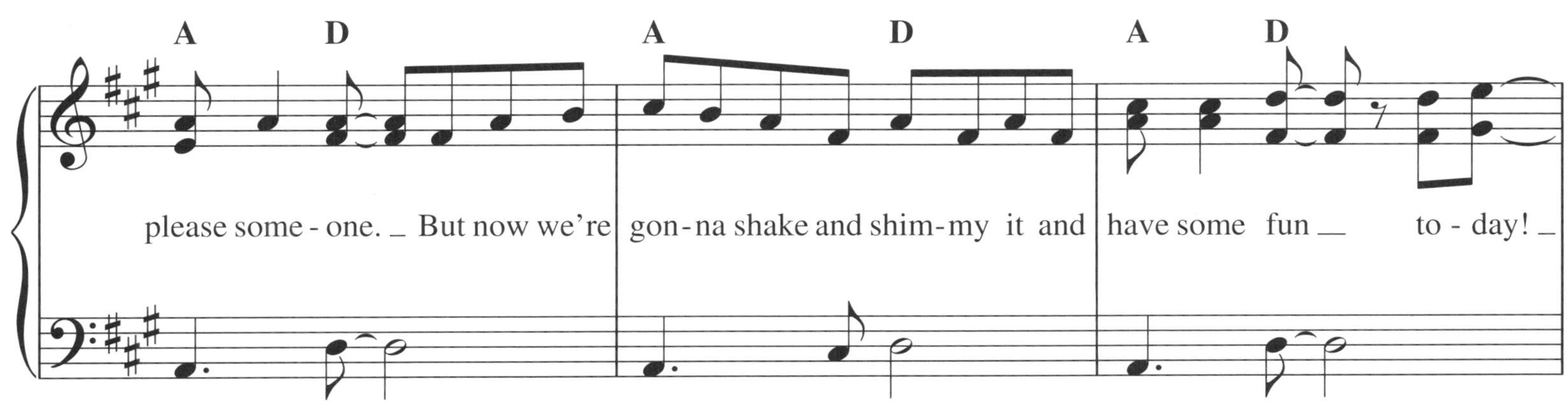
A D A D A D
please some - one. But now we're gon - na shake and shim - my it and have some fun to - day!

E Bm/E A/E E A D
'Cause you can't stop the mo - tion of the o - cean or the

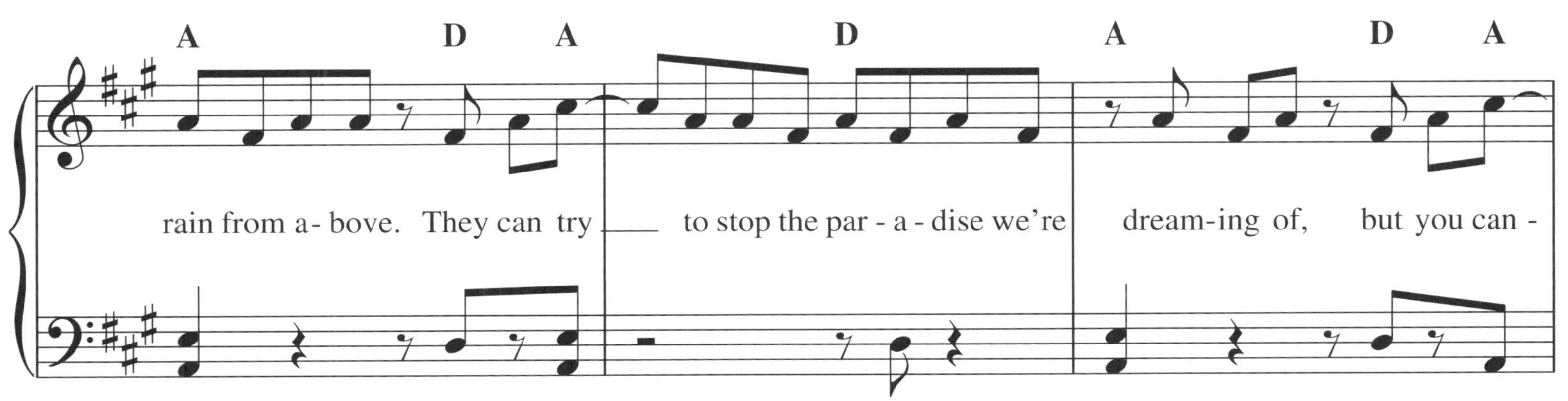
A D A D A D A
rain from a - bove. They can try to stop the par - a - dise we're dream - ing of, but you can -

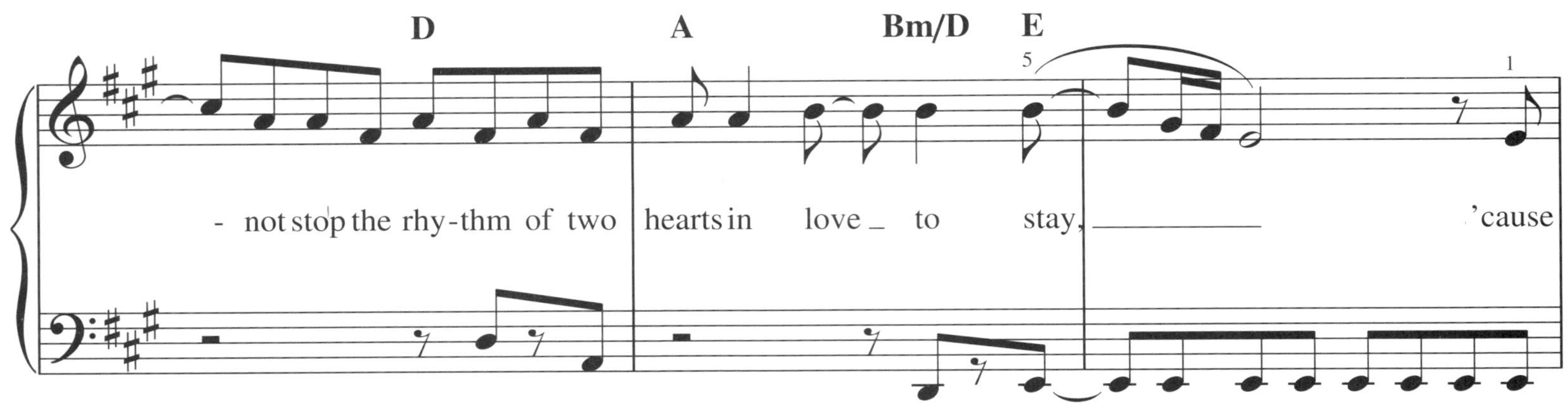

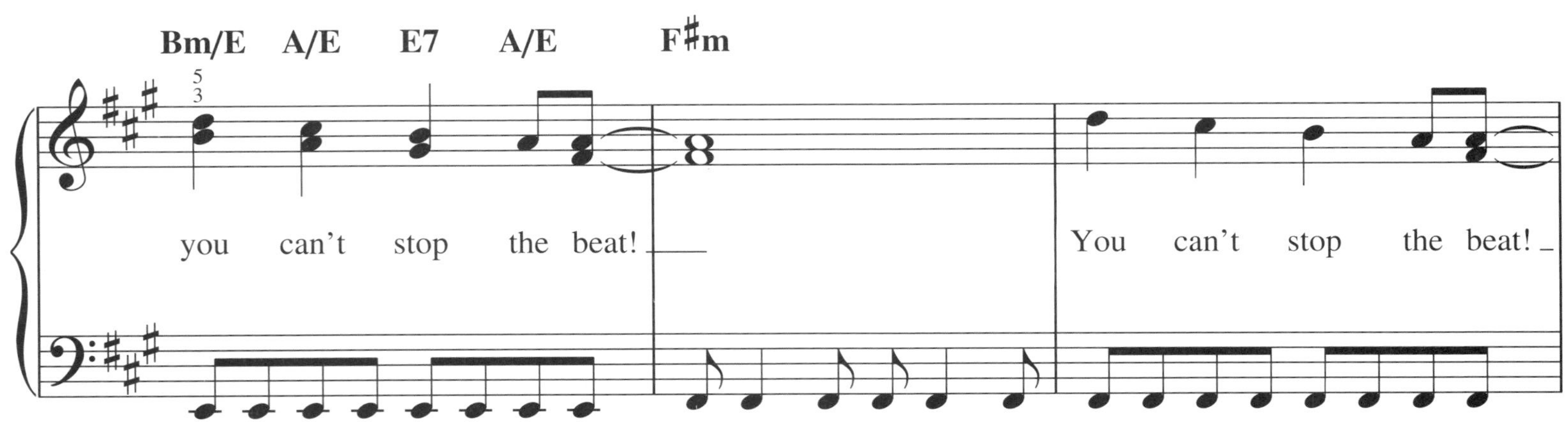

Additional Lyrics

4. Oh, oh, oh, you can't stop today
   As it comes speeding down the track.
   Child, yesterday is hist'ry and it's never coming back
   'Cause tomorrow is a brand new day
   And it don't know white from black,

IT'S NOT UNUSUAL

Words and Music by GORDON MILLS
and LES REED

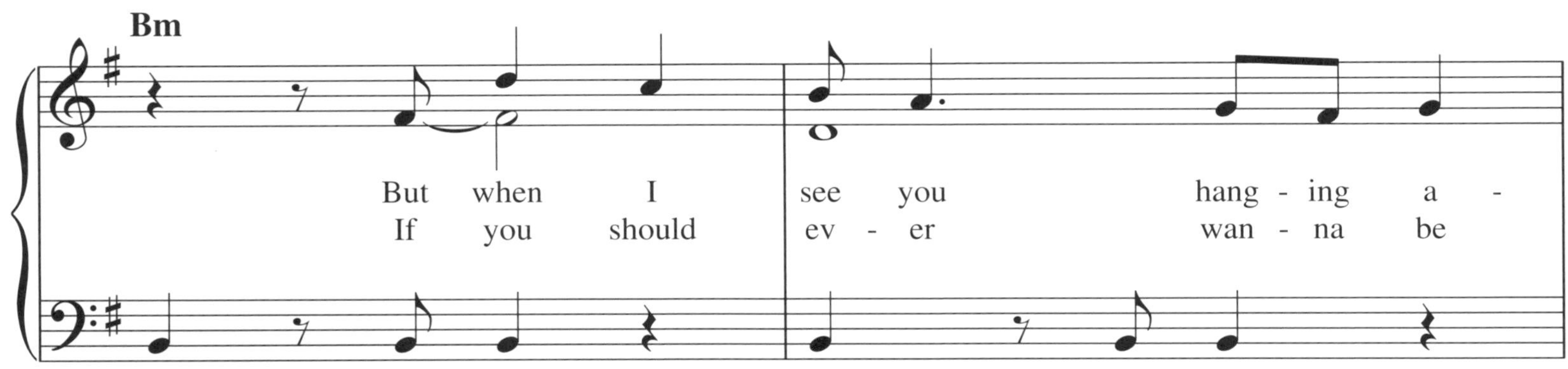

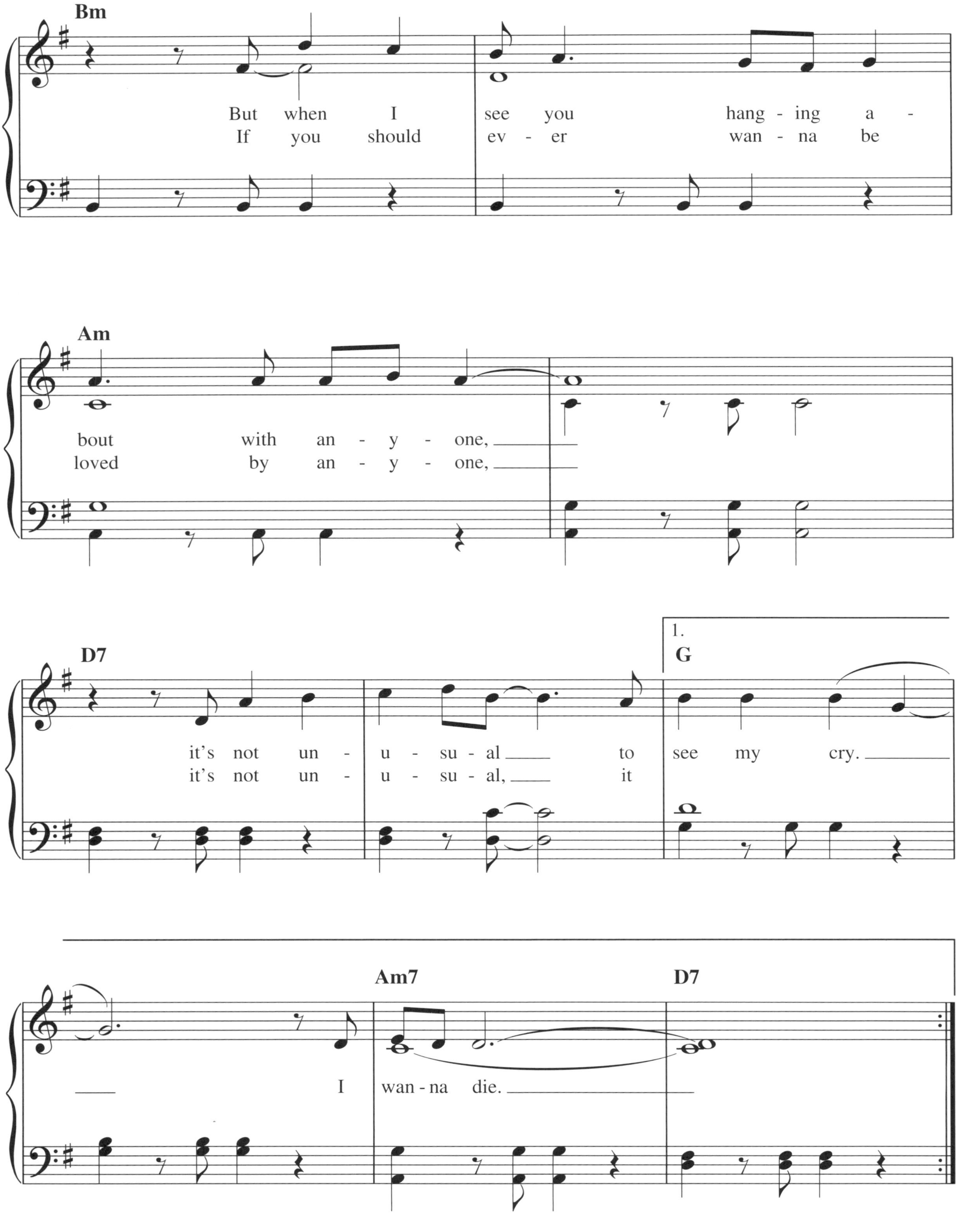

Am

bout with an - y - one, ___

loved by an - y - one, ___

D7

1.

G

it's not un - u - su - al ___ to see my cry. ___

it's not un - u - su - al, ___ it

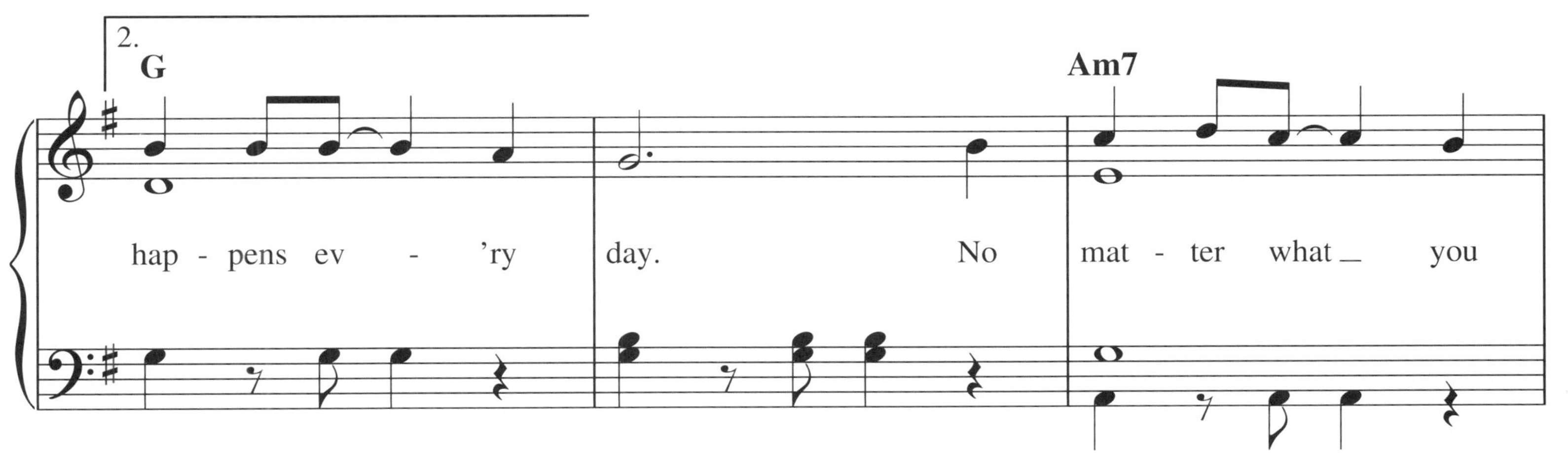
2.
G
Am7
hap - pens ev - 'ry day. No mat - ter what _ you

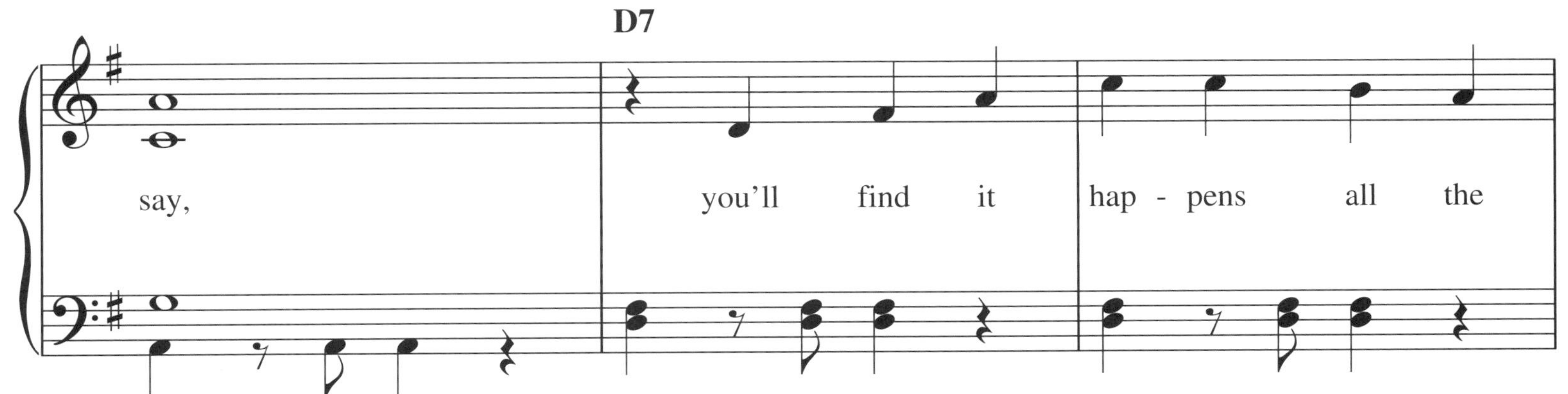
D7
say, you'll find it hap - pens all the

G
time.
Love will nev - er

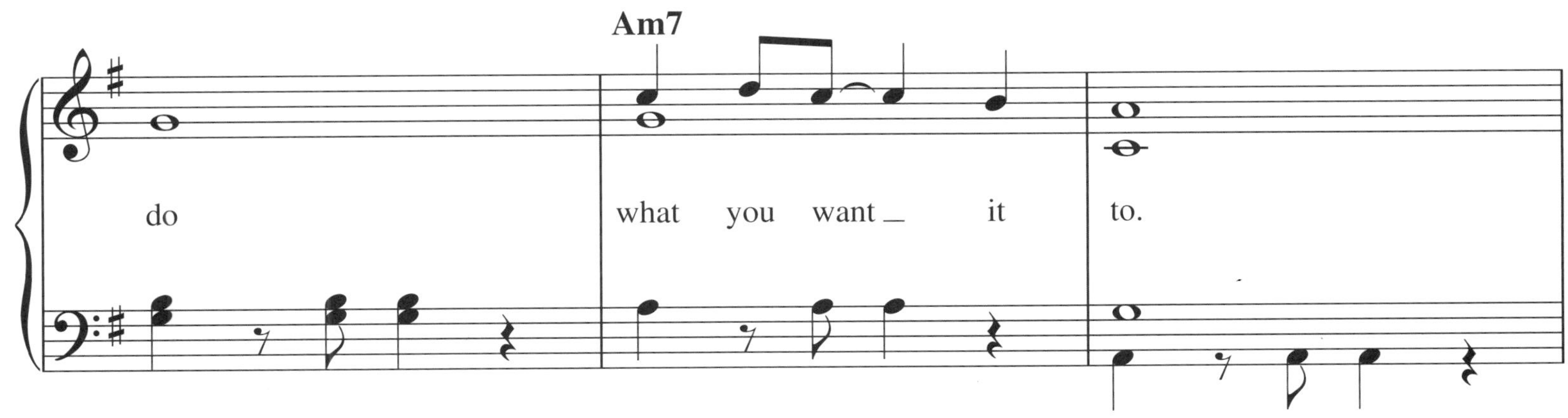
Am7
do what you want _ it to.

D7
Bm7
Why can't this cra - zy love be mine?
B♭7
Am7
D7
G
Am7
It's not un - u - su - al to be mad with an - y - one.
D7
G
It's not un - u - su - al to be

Am7
Bm
sad with an - y - one.
But if I

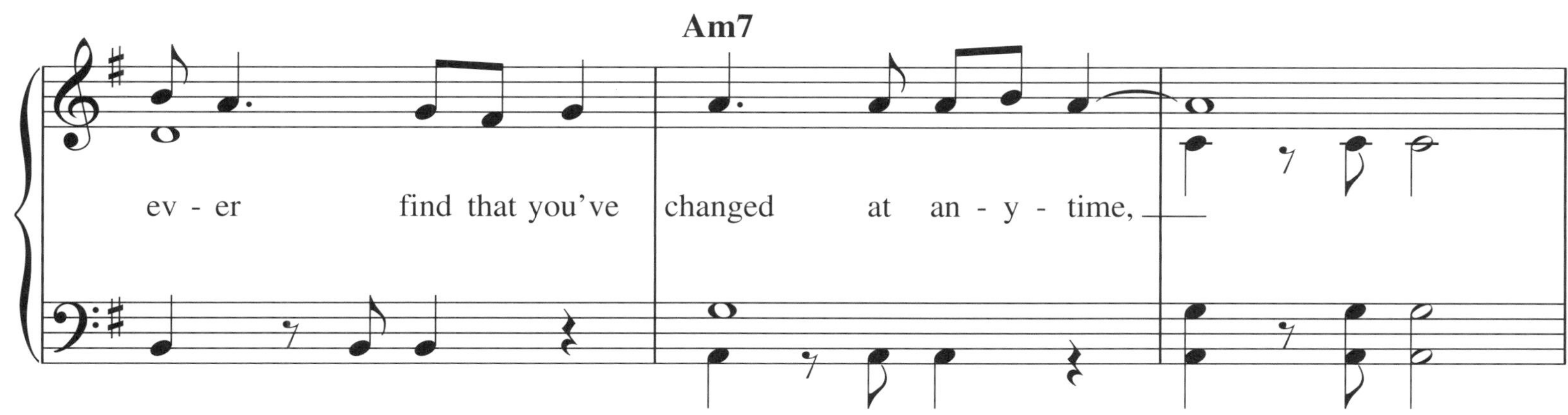
Am7
ev - er find that you've changed at an - y - time,

D7
G
it's not un - u - su - al to find that I'm in

Am7
D7
G
love with you.

SOMEWHERE

from WEST SIDE STORY

Lyrics by STEPHEN SONDHEIM
Music by LEONARD BERNSTEIN

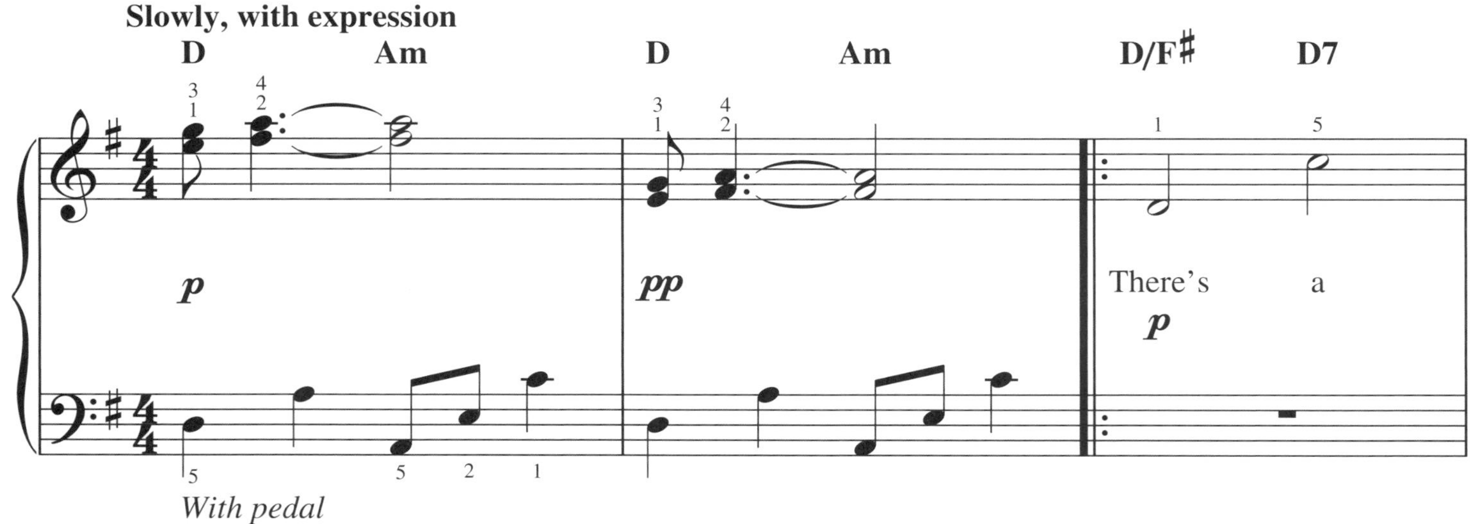

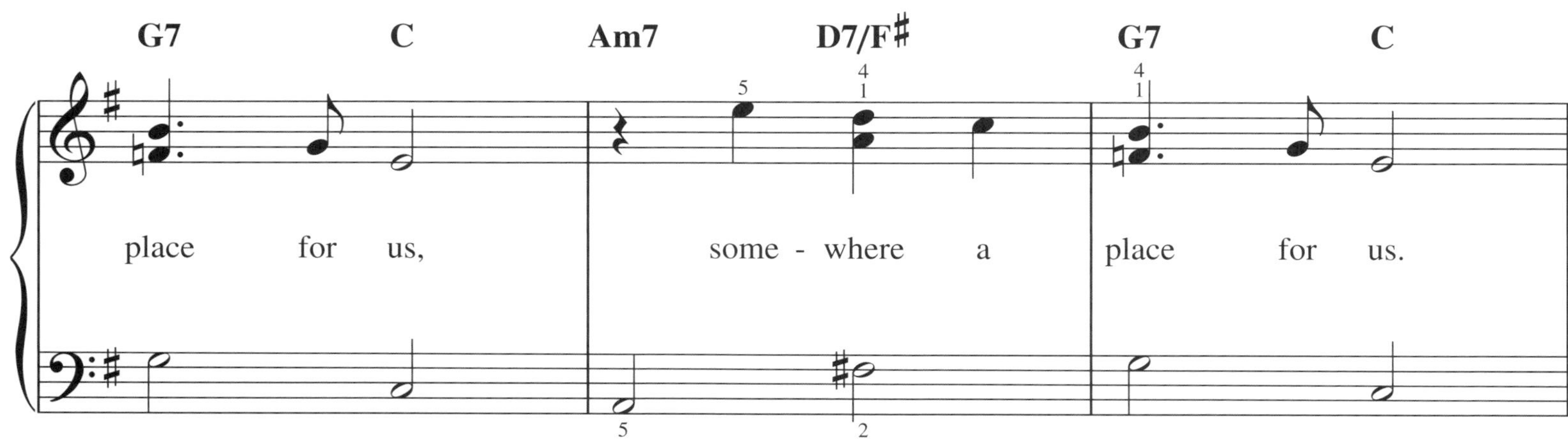

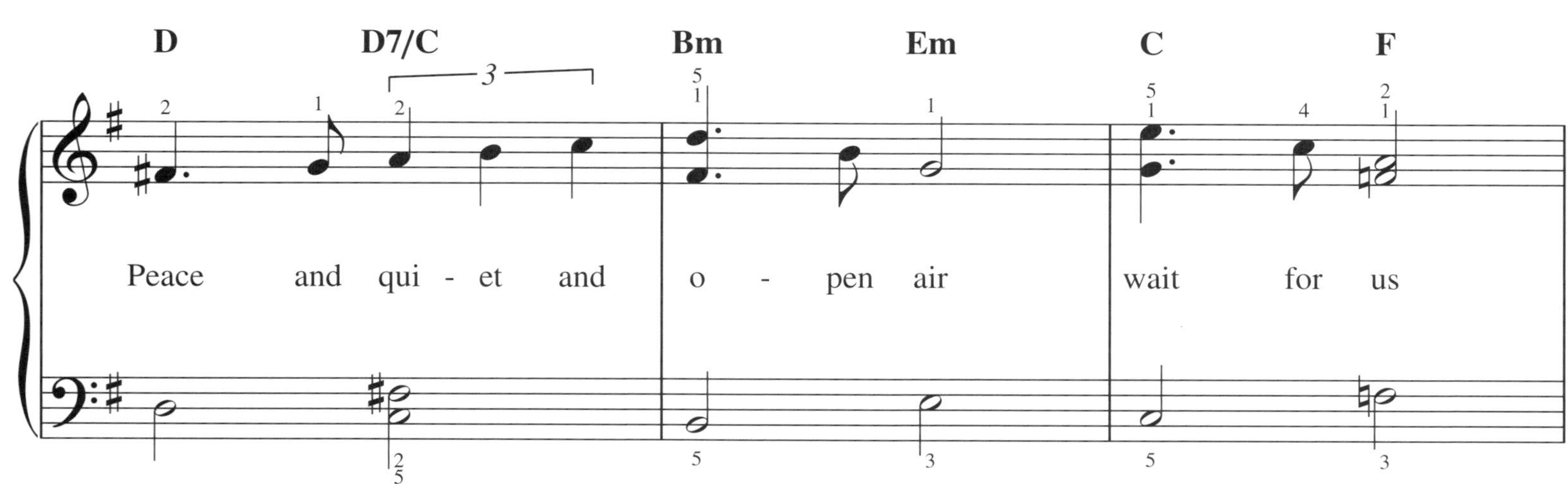

D
D/F♯
D7
G7
C
some - where.
There's a
p
time for us,
Am7
D7/F♯
G7
C
D
D7/C
some - day a
time for us.
Time to - geth - er with
Bm
E
C
F
Dm
B♭/D
time to spare,
time to learn,
time to care.
E♭
Cm
Some - day,
some - where

Gm
Am7
we'll find a new way of
liv - ing,
f
E♭
Cm6/E♭
B♭/D
we'll find a way of for -
giv - ing
p
A/C♯
A7
D/A
D7
some - where.
rit.
There's a
pp a tempo
G7
C
Am7
D7/F♯
G7
C
place for us,
a time and
place for us.

D
D7/C
Bm
Em
C
F
Hold my hand and we're half - way there.
Hold my hand and I'll
cresc.
Dm
B♭
E♭
Cm
take you there,
some-how,
some-day,
f
1.
G
G7/F
C/E
Am7
2.
G
G7/F
some - where.
some - where.
C/E
Am7
Slower
G
pp

RUN THE WORLD
(Girls)

Words and Music by BEYONCÉ KNOWLES,
DAVE TAYLOR, THOMAS WESLEY PENTZ,
NICK VAN DE WALL, ADIDJA PALMER
and TERIUS NASH

run the world? Girls, girls.
Some of them men think they freak this
It's hot in here. D.J., don't be scared

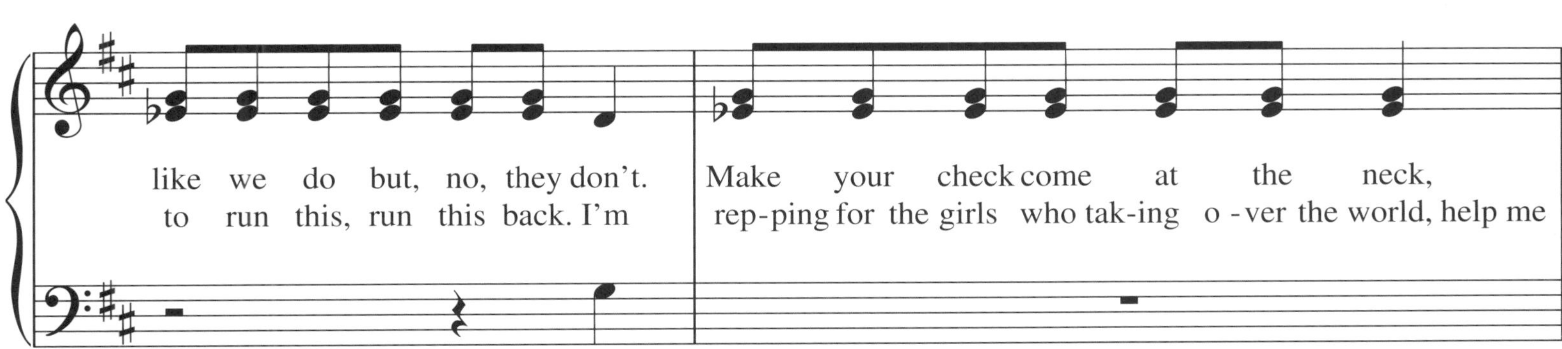
like we do but, no, they don't. Make your check come at the neck,
to run this, run this back. I'm rep-ping for the girls who tak-ing o-ver the world, help me

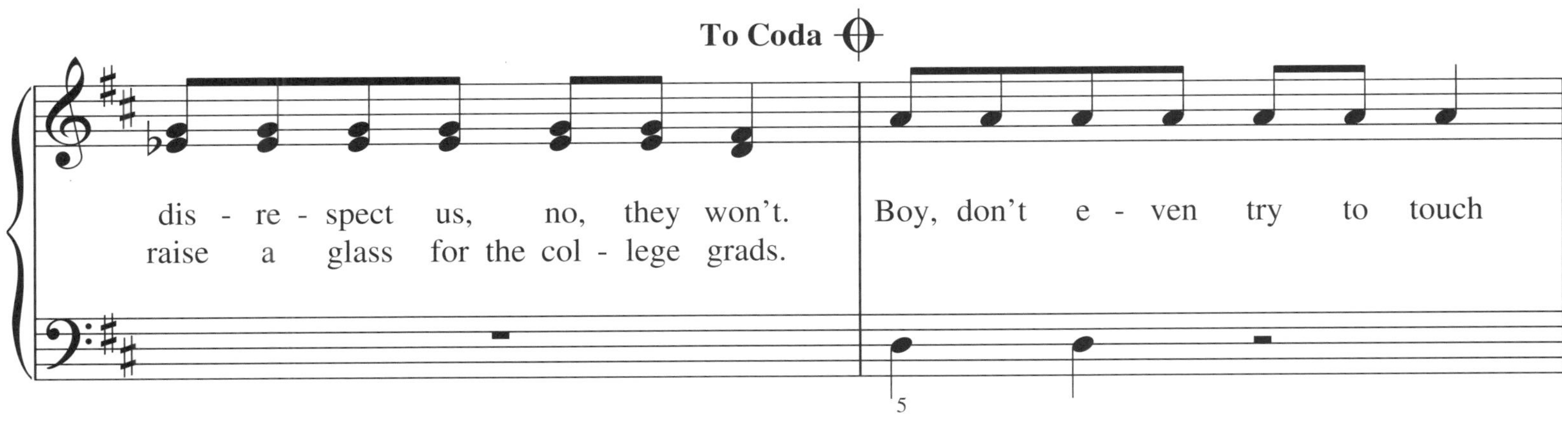
To Coda
dis-re-spect us, no, they won't. Boy, don't e-ven try to touch
raise a glass for the col-lege grads.

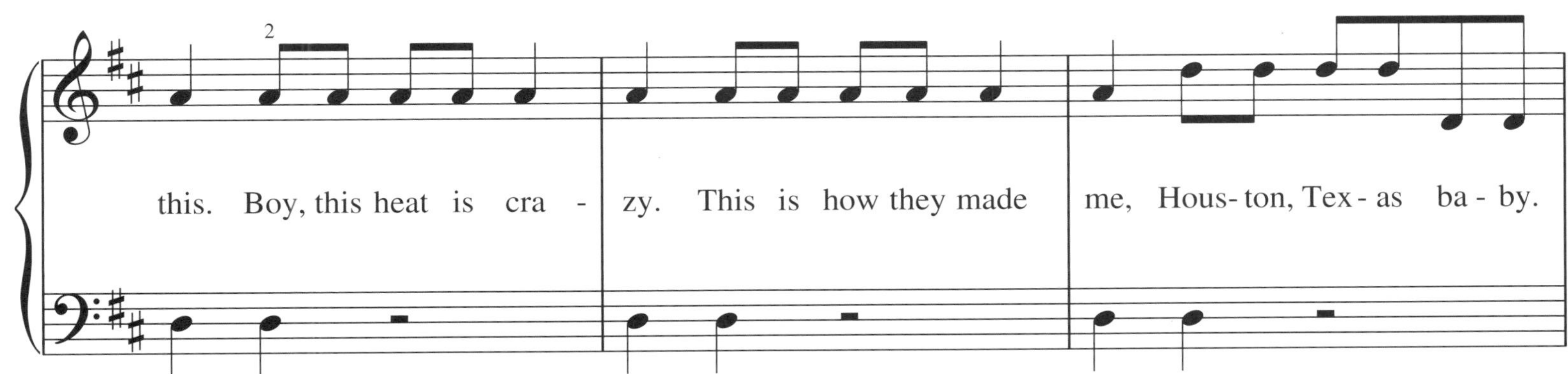
this. Boy, this heat is cra-zy. This is how they made me, Hous-ton, Tex-as ba-by.

E♭
This goes out to all my girls that's in the club rock - ing the lat -
D
E♭
est. Who will buy it for them - selves and get more mon - ey lat -
D
er. I think I need a bar - ber, none of these peo - ple can fade
me. I'm so good with this, I re - mind you, I'm so hood with this.
E♭
Boy, I'm just play -
5
1
4

D
E♭
D
E♭
D
B♭
ing. Come here, ba - by. Hope you still like me. F. you, pay me. My per -

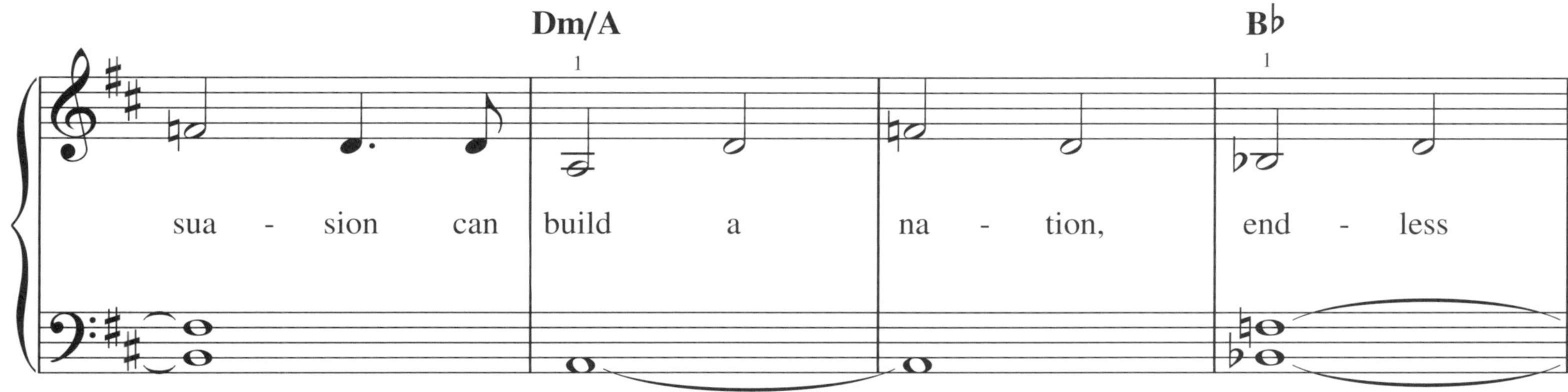
Dm/A
B♭
sua - sion can build a na - tion, end - less

D/A
N.C.
pow - er, with our love ___ we can de - vour. ___ You'll do ___ an - y -

D.S. al Coda
thing ___ for me. ___ Who run the world? _ Girls, girls. Who

CODA
E♭
D
An - y - one roll - ing, I'll let you know what time it is, check.
4

E♭
D
You can't hold me, I work my nine - to - five and I cut my check.

E♭maj7
D
This goes out to all the wom - en get-ting it in, get on your grind.

E♭maj7
D
To oth - er men that res - pect what I do, please ac - cept my shine.

Boy, I know you love it, how we're smart e - nough to make these mil - lions,

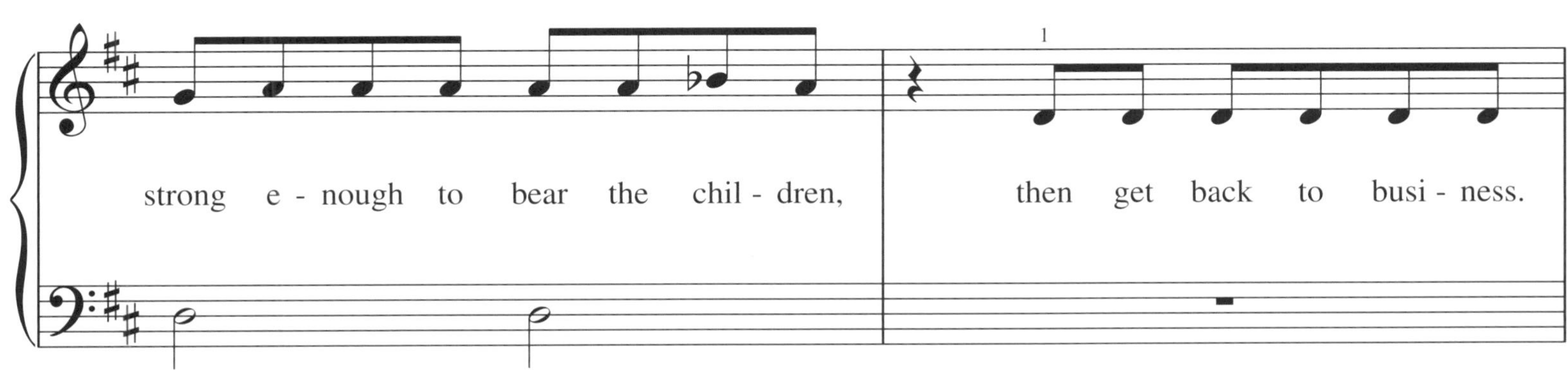
strong e - nough to bear the chil - dren, then get back to busi - ness.

E♭
D
E♭
See, you bet - ter not play me. Don't come here, ba -

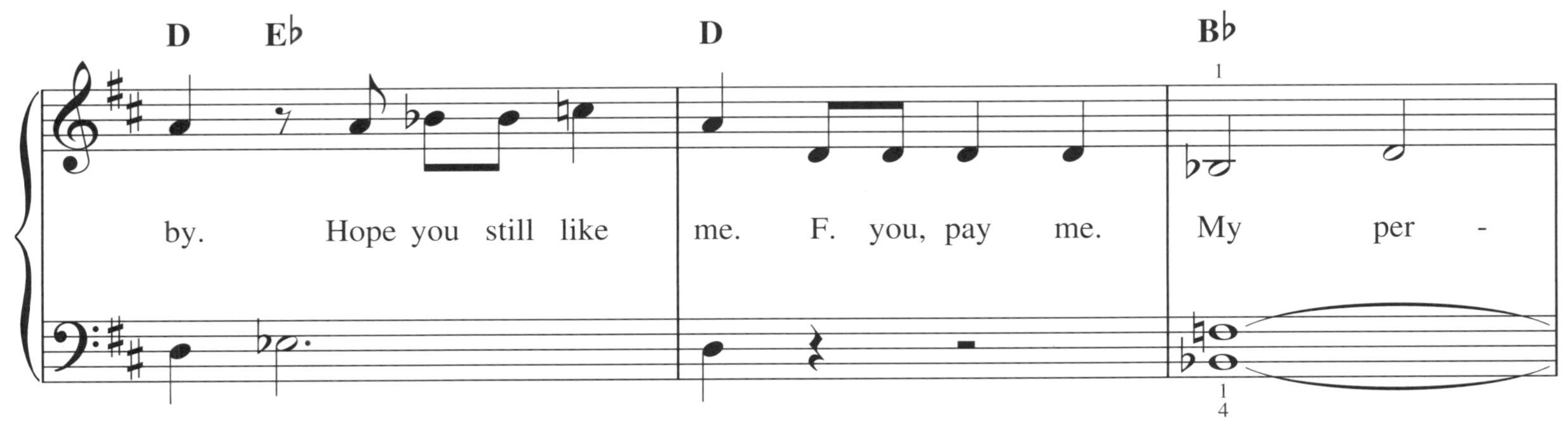
D
E♭
D
B♭
by. Hope you still like me. F. you, pay me. My per -

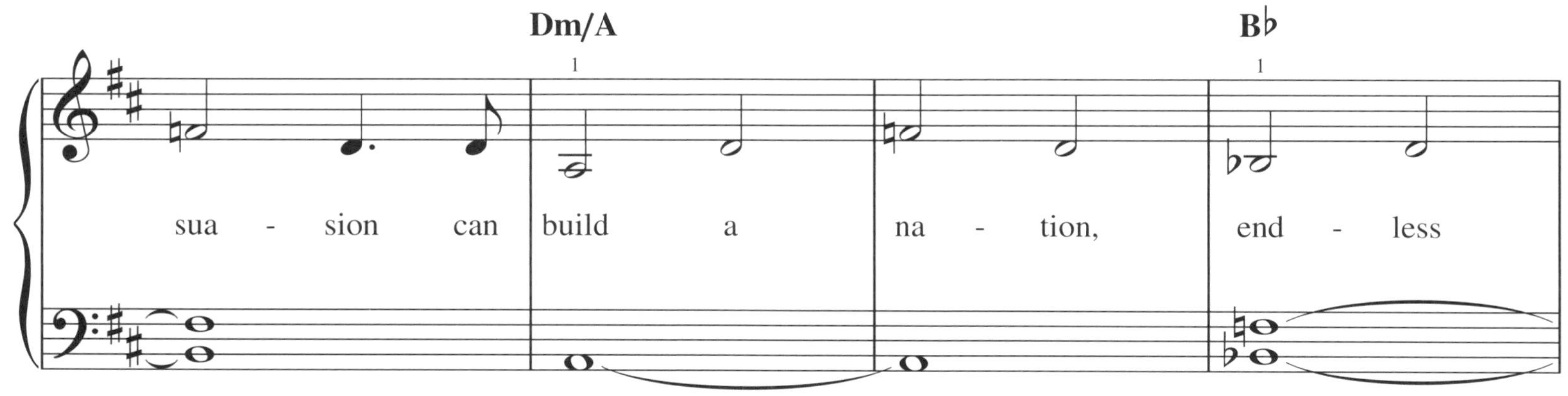
Dm/A
B♭
sua - sion can build a na - tion, end - less

D/A
N.C.
pow - er, with our love we can de - vour. You'll do an - y -

thing for me. Who run the world? Girls, girls. Who

run the world? Girls, girls. Who run this moth - er? Girls! Who run this moth - er? Girls! Who

1
run the world? Girls, girls. Who run the world? Girls! Who are we?

B♭
D/A
What we run? The world! Who
1
4
1
5

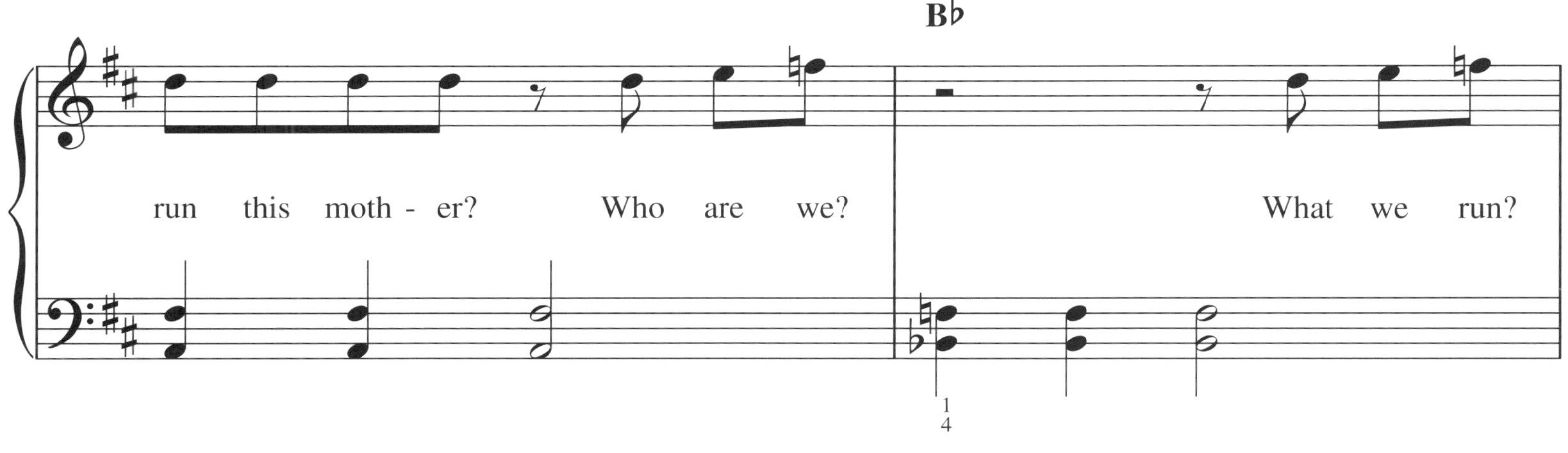
B♭
run this moth - er? Who are we? What we run?
1
4

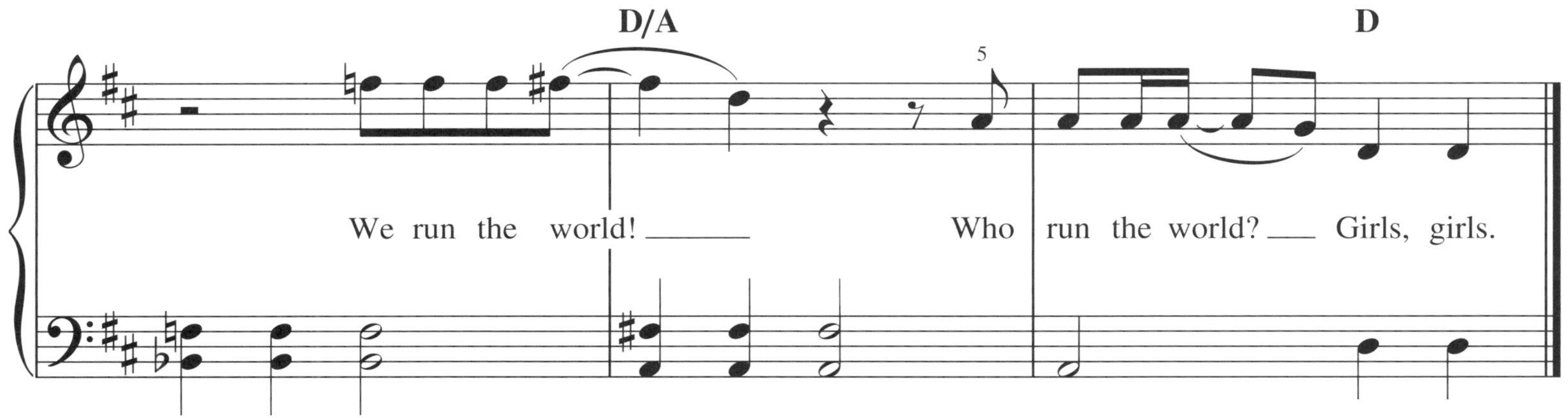
D/A
D
5
We run the world! Who run the world? Girls, girls.

FIX YOU

Words and Music by GUY BERRYMAN,
JON BUCKLAND, WILL CHAMPION
and CHRIS MARTIN

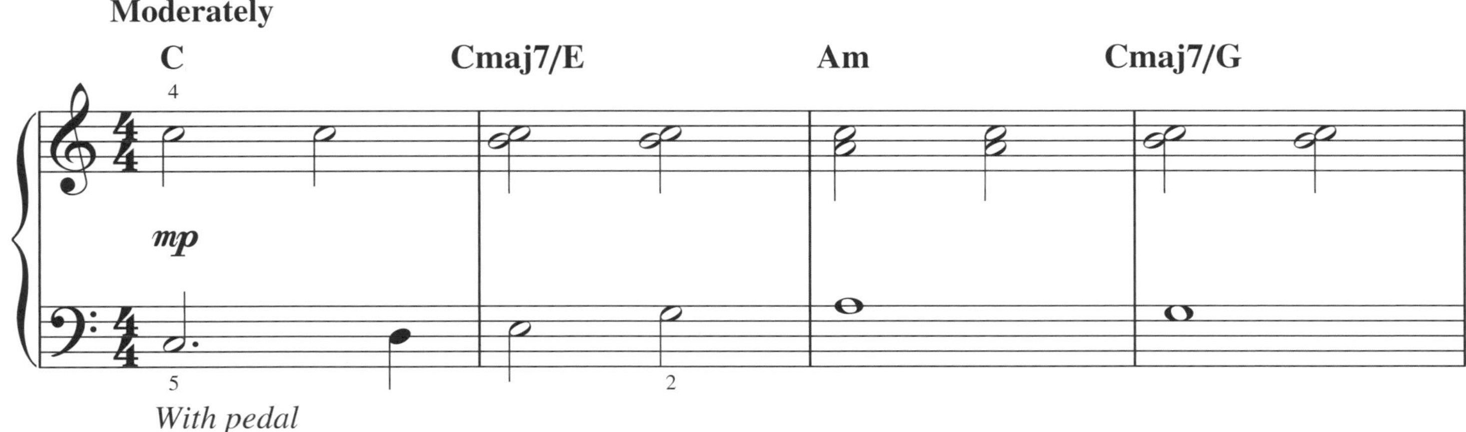

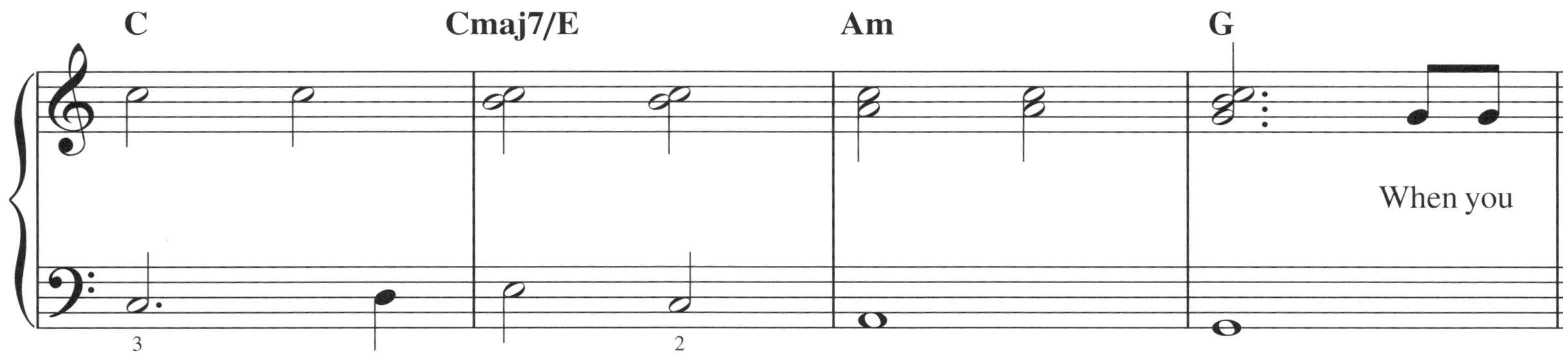

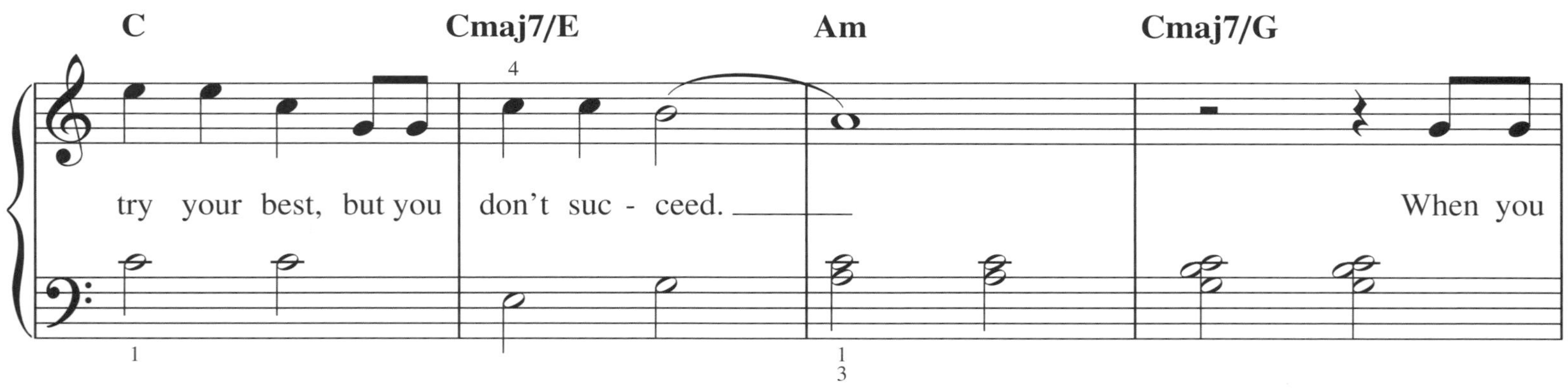

C
Cmaj7/E
Am
Cmaj7/G
feel so tired, but you can't sleep.
Stuck in re -

C
C/E
Am
Cmaj7/G
verse.
And the

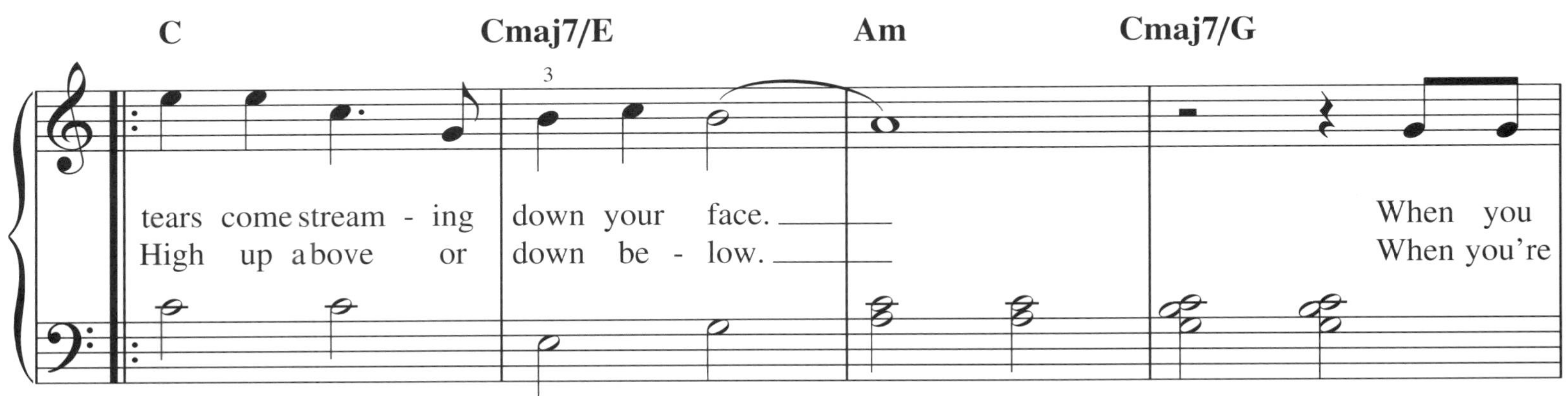
C
Cmaj7/E
Am
Cmaj7/G
tears come stream - ing down your face.
When you
High up above or down be - low.
When you're

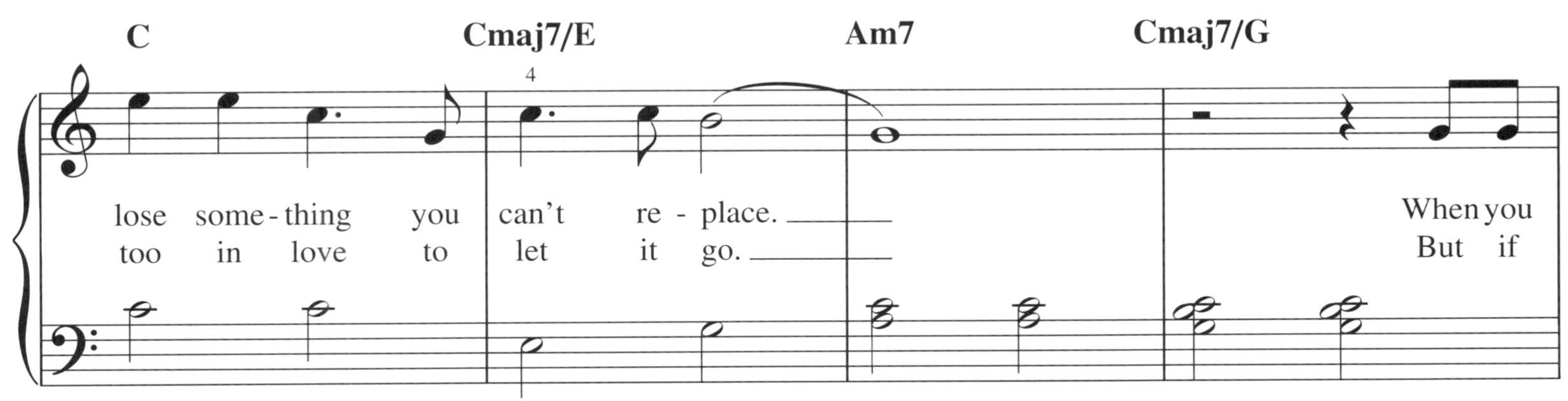
C
Cmaj7/E
Am7
Cmaj7/G
lose some - thing you can't re - place.
When you
too in love to let it go.
But if

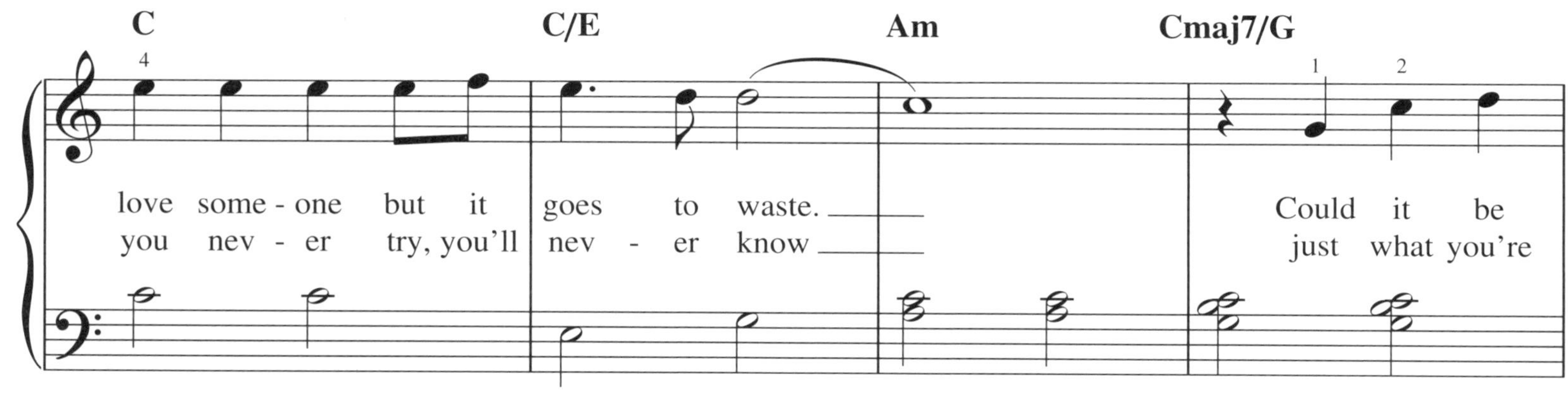
C
C/E
Am
Cmaj7/G
love some - one but it goes to waste.
you nev - er try, you'll nev - er know
Could it be
just what you're

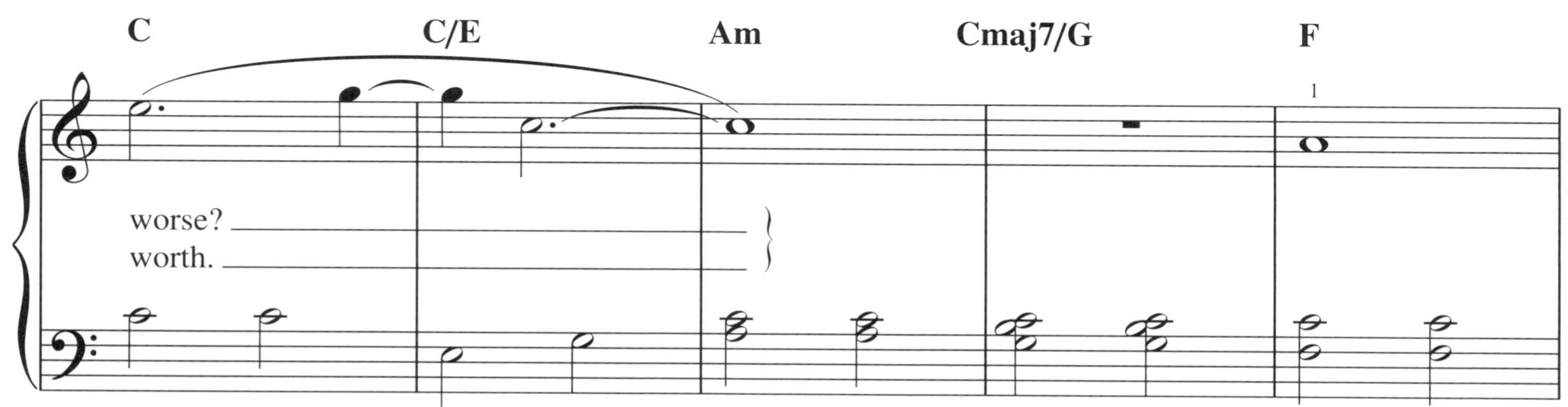
C
C/E
Am
Cmaj7/G
F
worse?
worth.

Gsus
G
F
Lights will guide you home and ig -

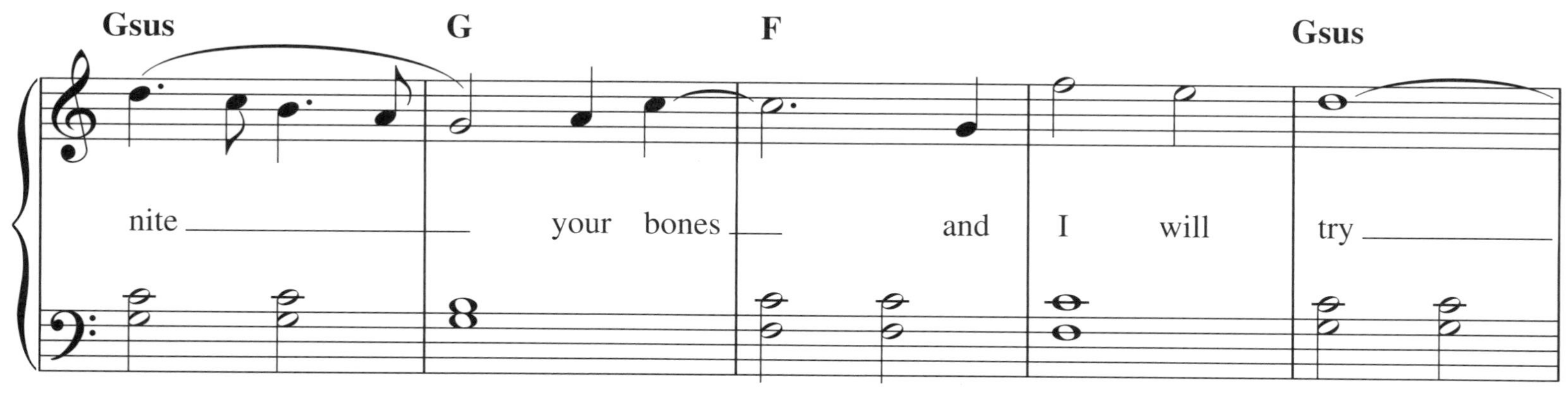
Gsus
G
F
Gsus
nite your bones and I will try

1.
G
C
Cmaj7/E
Am
1
to fix you.

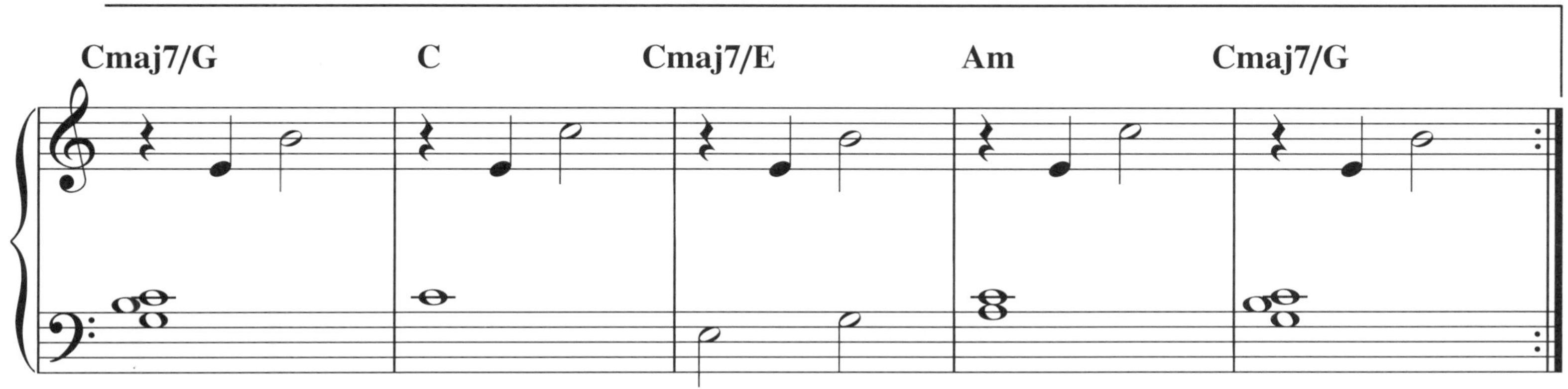
Cmaj7/G
C
Cmaj7/E
Am
Cmaj7/G

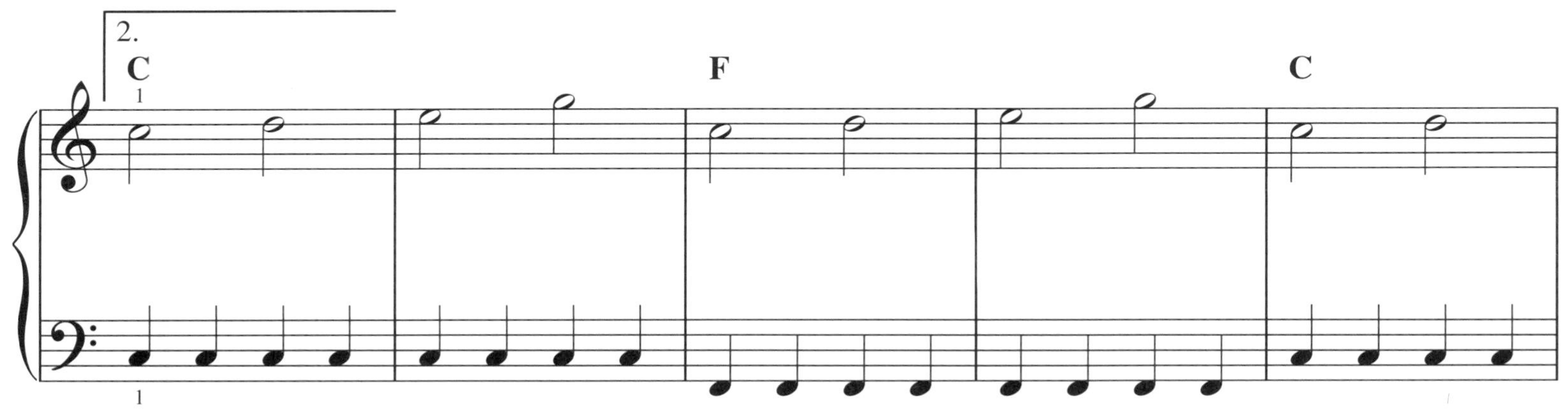
2.
C
F
C
1
1

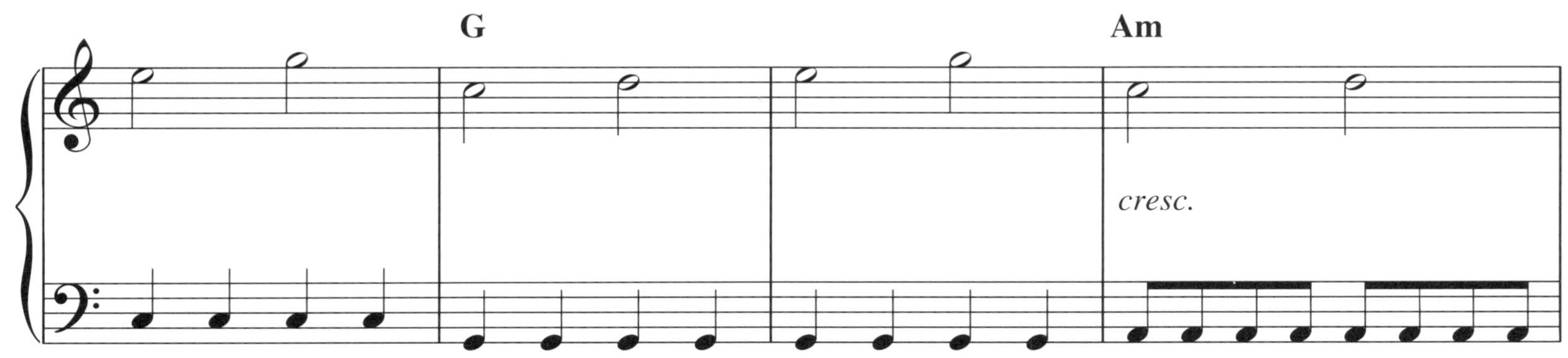
G
Am
cresc.

F
C

G
C
f

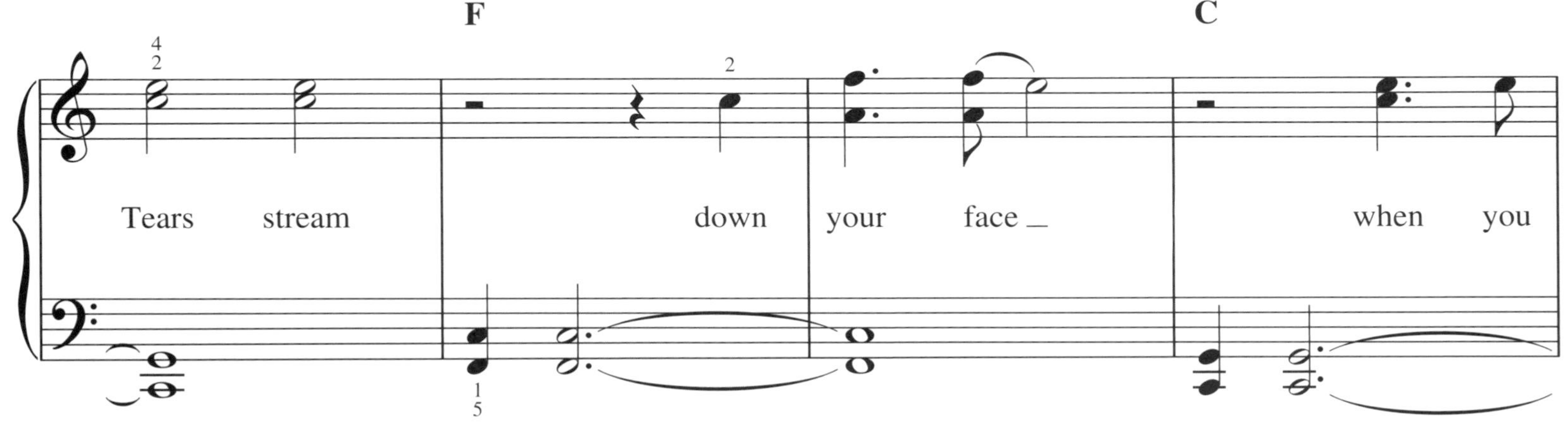
F
C
Tears stream down your face _ when you

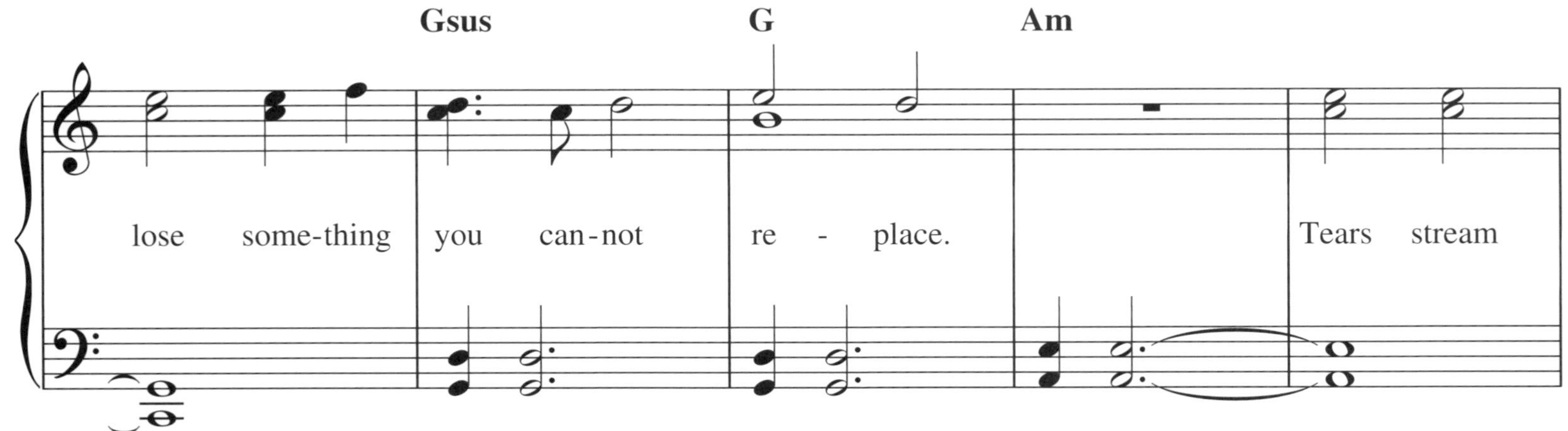
Gsus
G
Am
lose some-thing you can-not re - place. Tears stream

F
C
down your face and I...
Gsus
G
C
F
Tears stream down
C
Em7
your face.
I prom - ise you I will learn from my
Am
F
mis - takes.
Tears stream down your face and

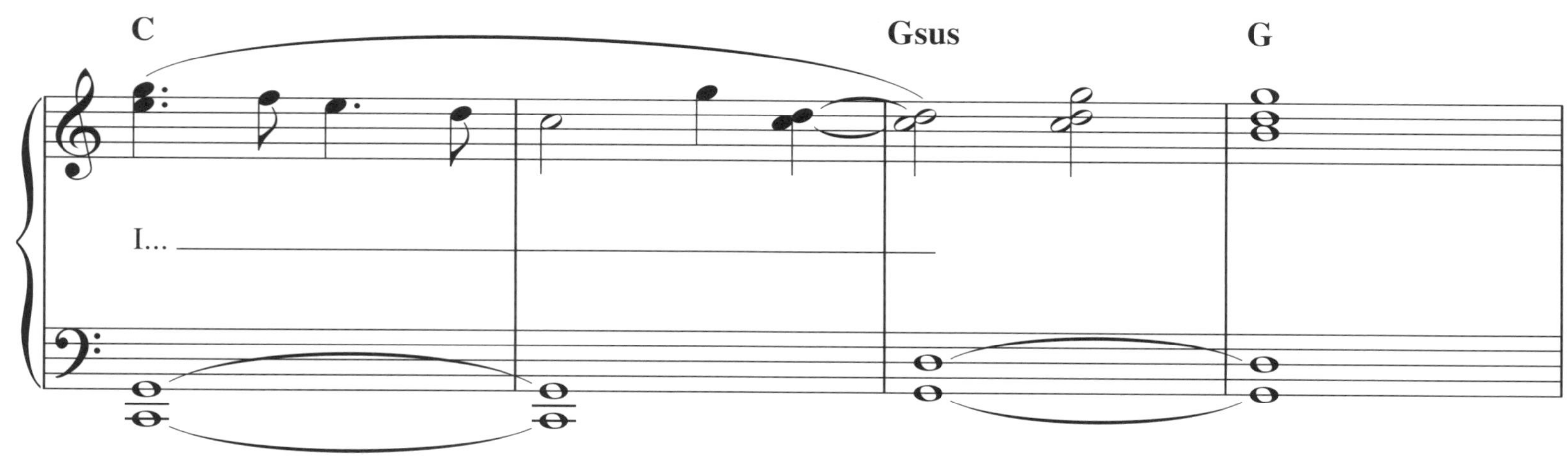
C
Gsus
G
I...

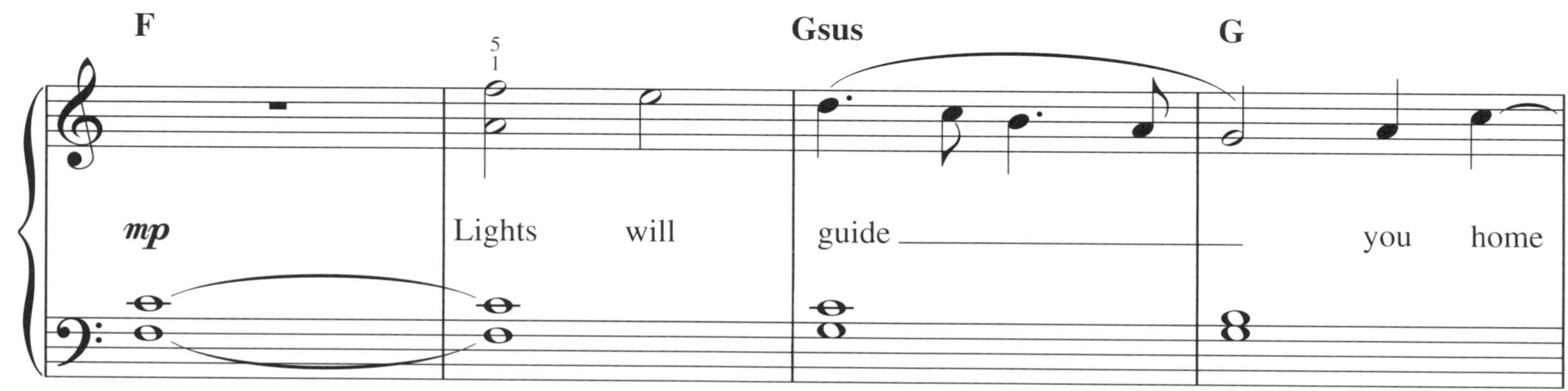
F
Gsus
G
5
1
mp
Lights will guide you home

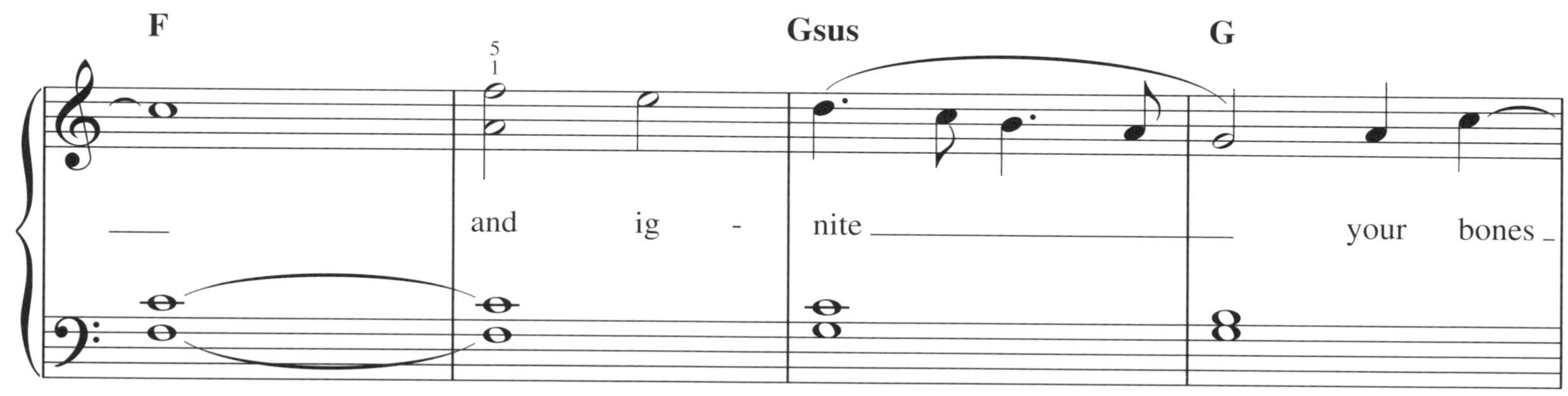
F
Gsus
G
5
1
and ig - nite your bones

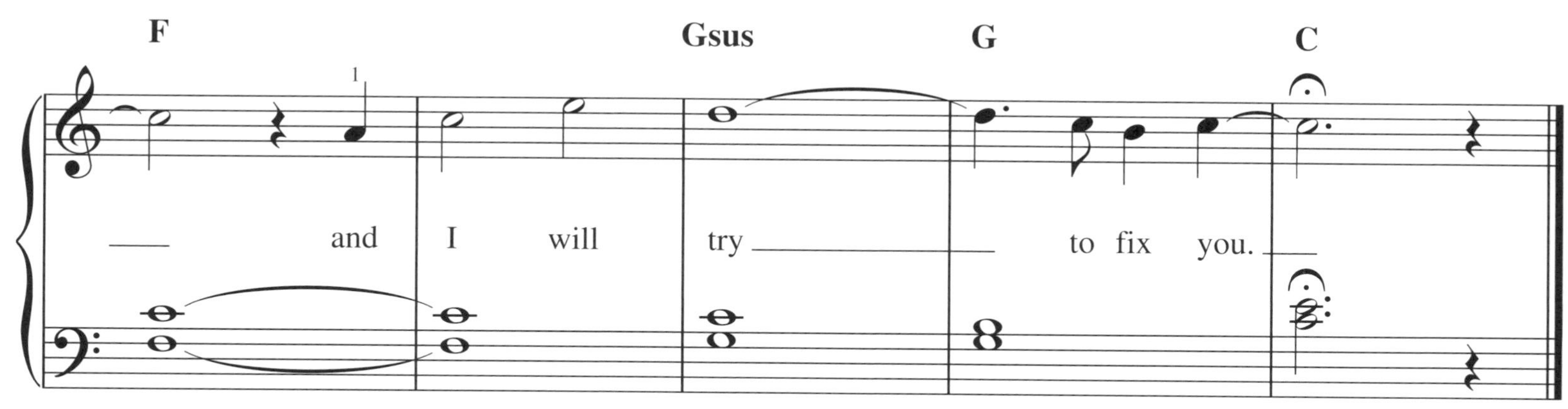
F
Gsus
G
C
1
and I will try to fix you.

TONIGHT

from WEST SIDE STORY

Lyrics by STEPHEN SONDHEIM
Music by LEONARD BERNSTEIN

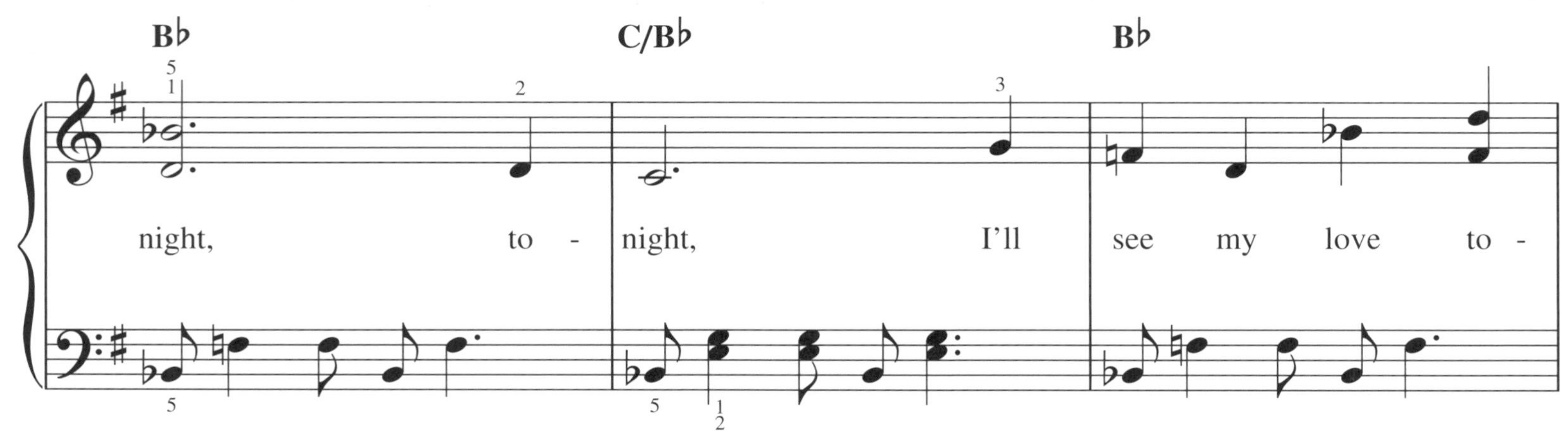

B♭
C/B♭
B♭
night, to - night, I'll see my love to -

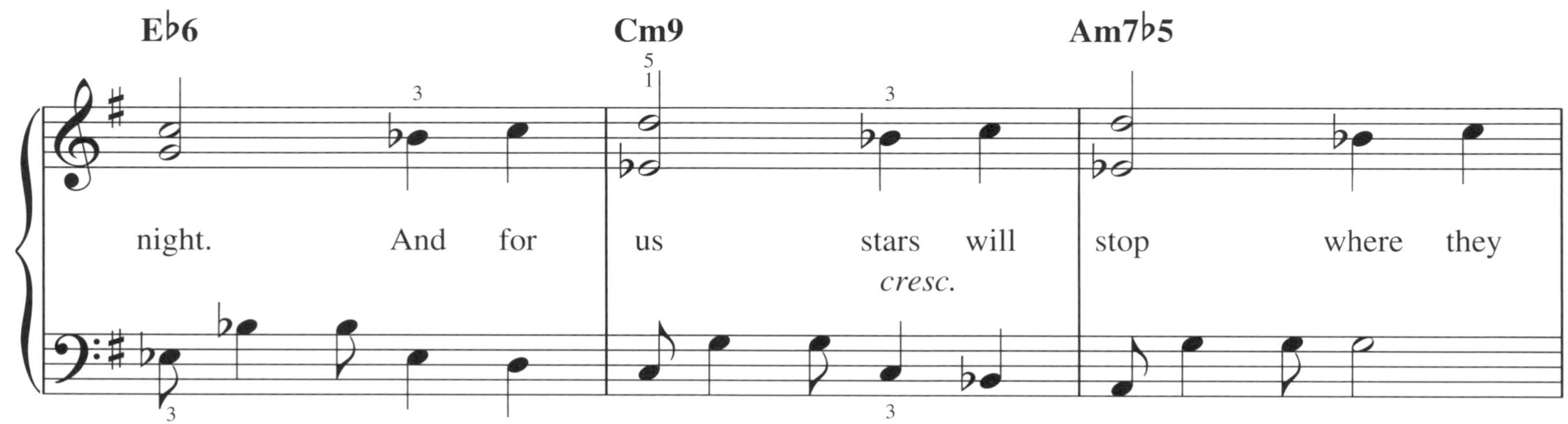

E♭6
Cm9
Am7♭5
night. And for us stars will stop where they
cresc.

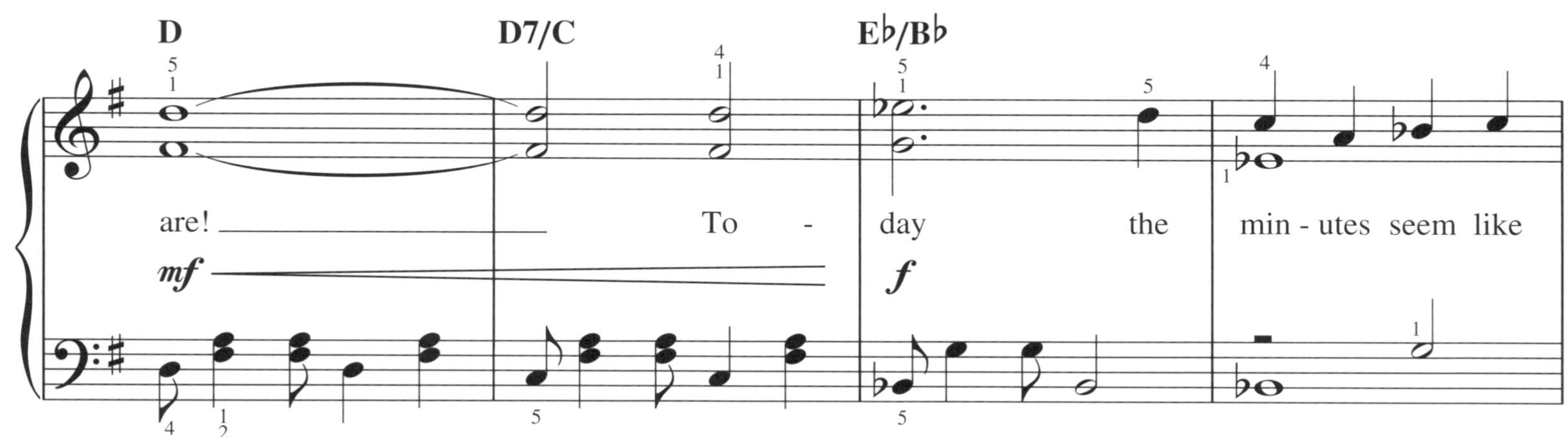

D
D7/C
E♭/B♭
are! To - day the min - utes seem like
mf
f

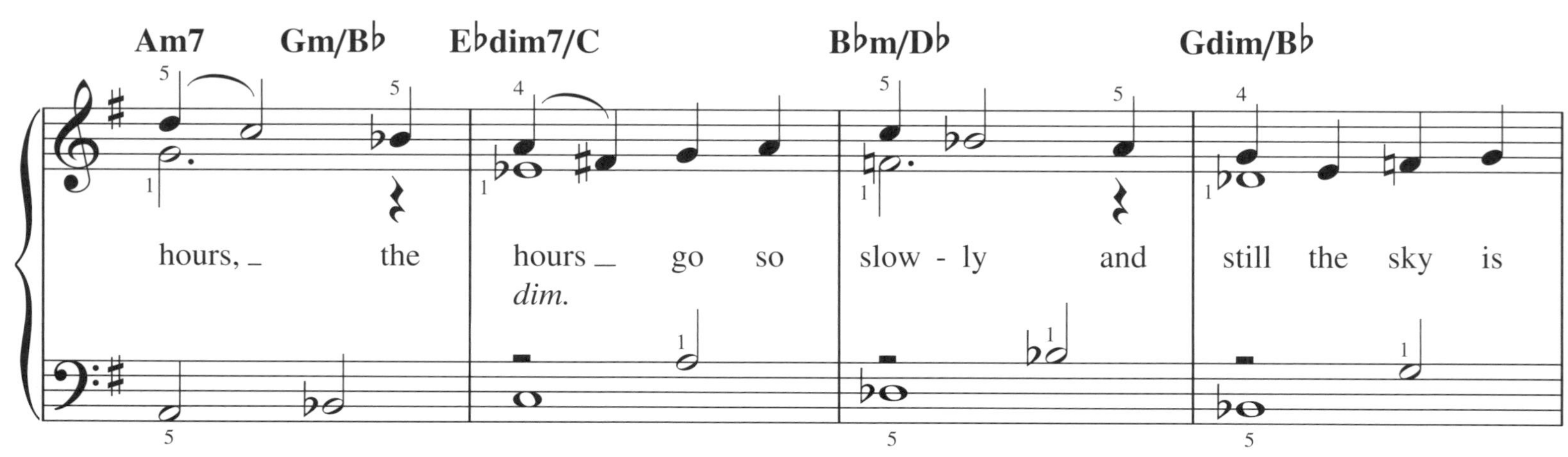

Am7
Gm/B♭
E♭dim7/C
B♭m/D♭
Gdim/B♭
hours, the hours go so slow - ly and still the sky is
dim.

A
E♭7
G/D
light.
O
moon,
grow
pp
A/G
G
Em7
bright,
and
make
this
end - less
day
end - less
Bm
Am7
D7sus/A
1.
Gmaj7
Em7
Am9
D7
night,
to -
night!
To -
mf
f
2.
Gmaj7
Em7
Cmaj9
G/B
G/A
G(add9)
night!
f
rit.
ff

LAST FRIDAY NIGHT
(T.G.I.F.)

Words and Music by LUKASZ GOTTWALD, MAX MARTIN, BONNIE McKEE and KATY PERRY

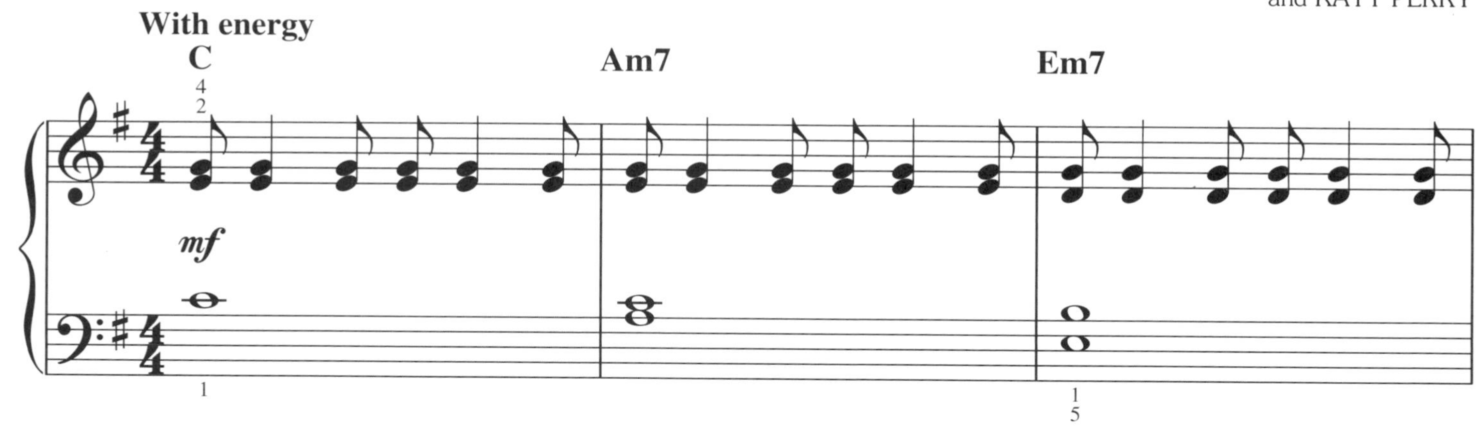

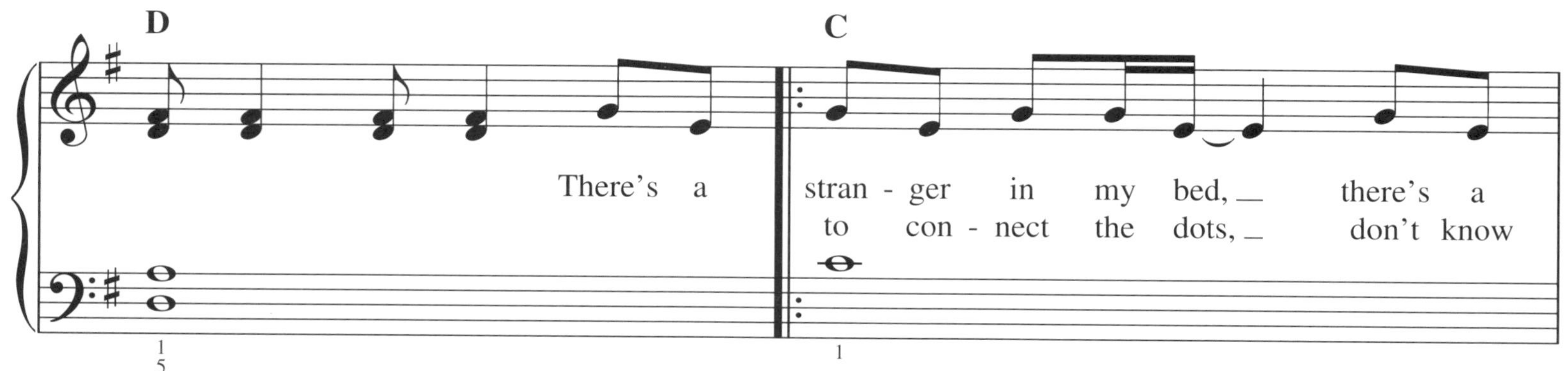

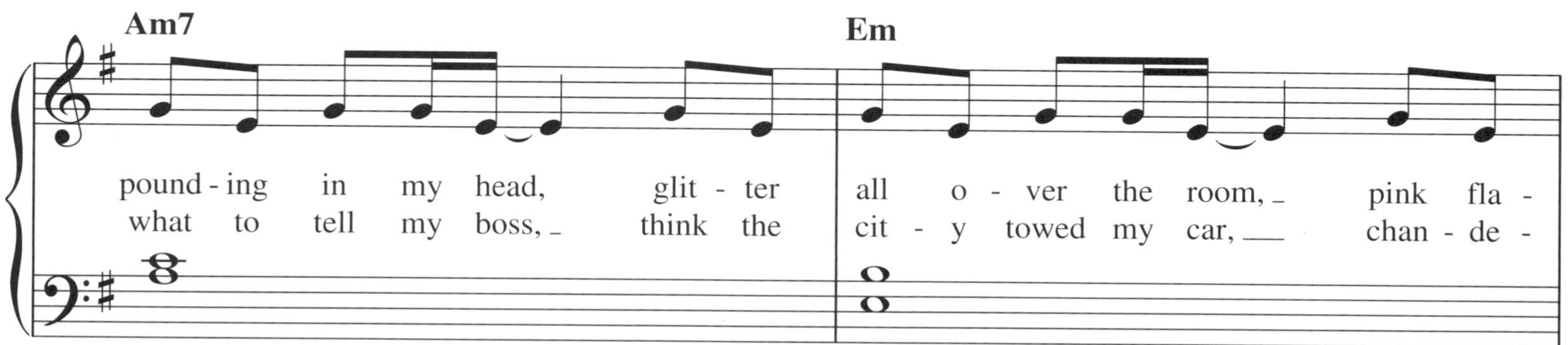

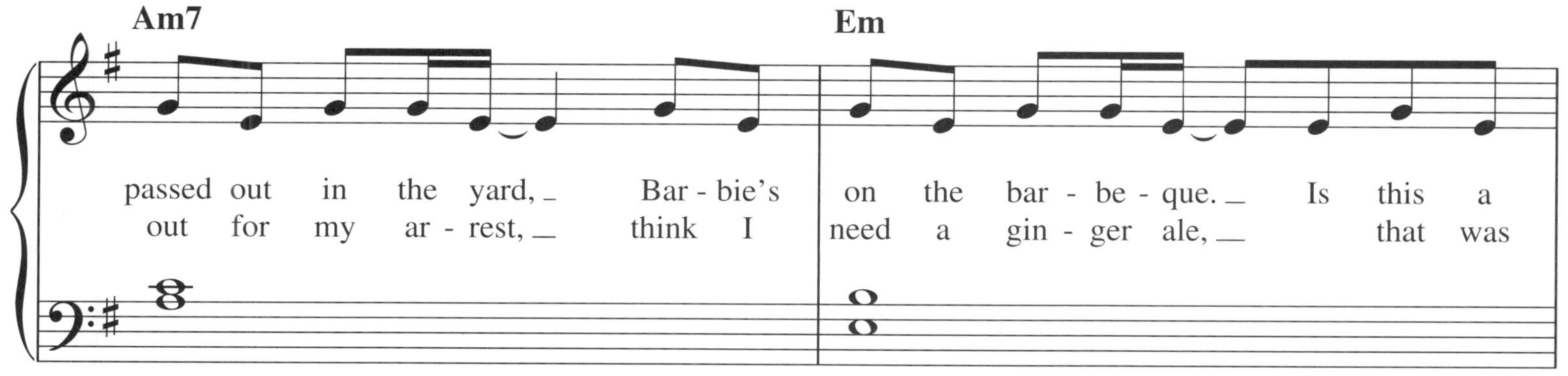
Am7
Em
passed out in the yard, Bar - bie's on the bar - be - que. Is this a
out for my ar - rest, think I need a gin - ger ale, that was

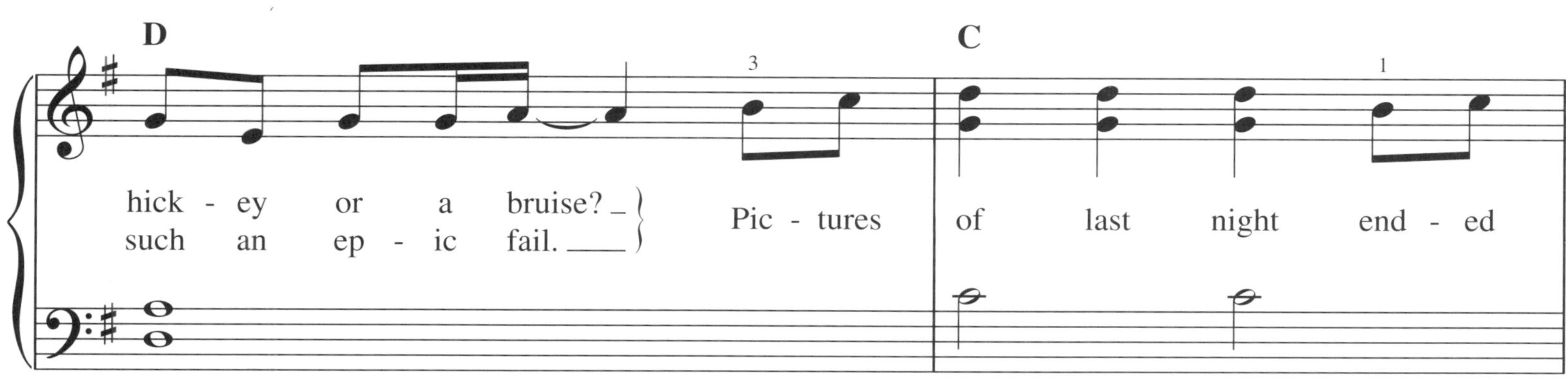
D
C
3
1
hick - ey or a bruise?
such an ep - ic fail.
Pic - tures of last night end - ed

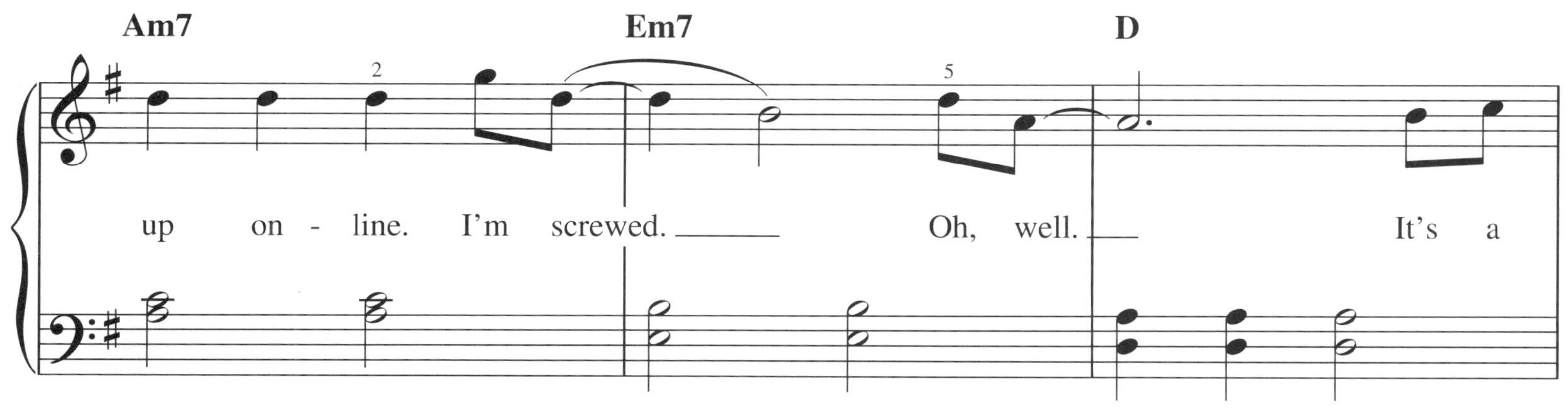
Am7
Em7
D
2
5
up on - line. I'm screwed. Oh, well. It's a

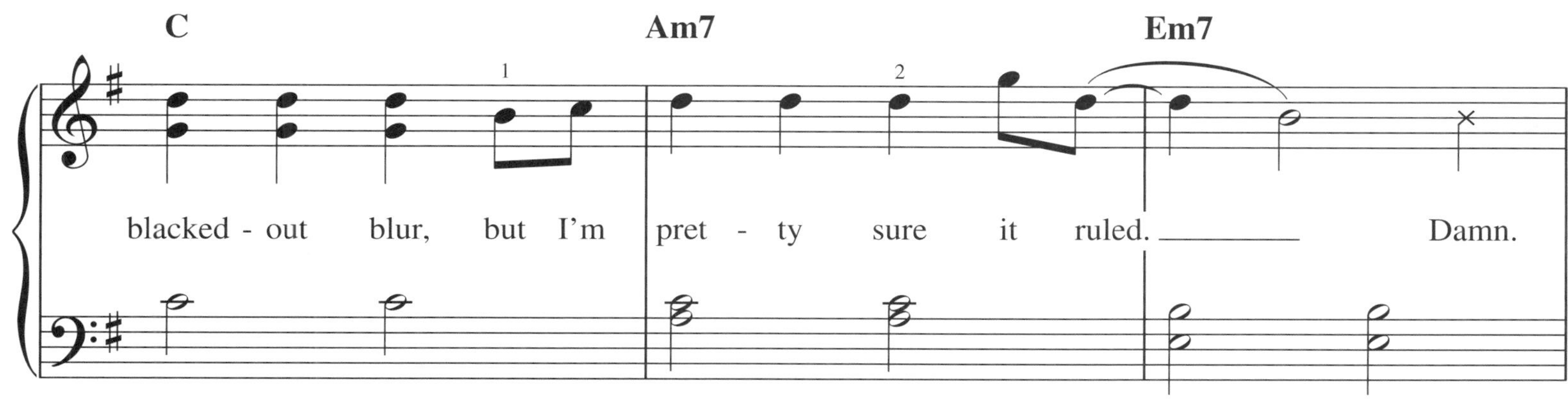
C
Am7
Em7
1
2
blacked - out blur, but I'm pret - ty sure it ruled. Damn.

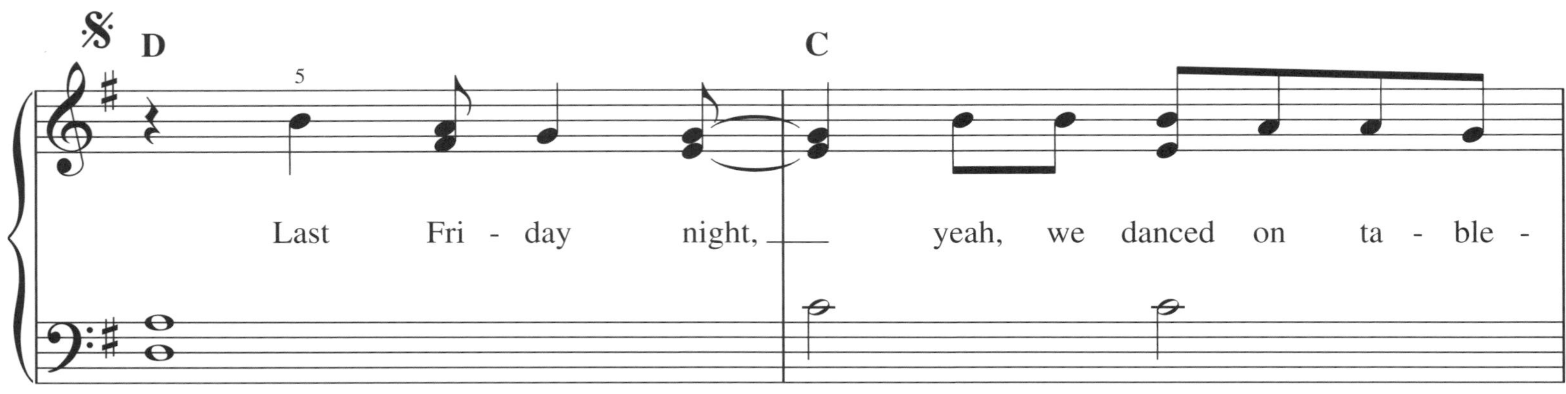
D
C
5
Last Fri - day night, yeah, we danced on ta - ble -

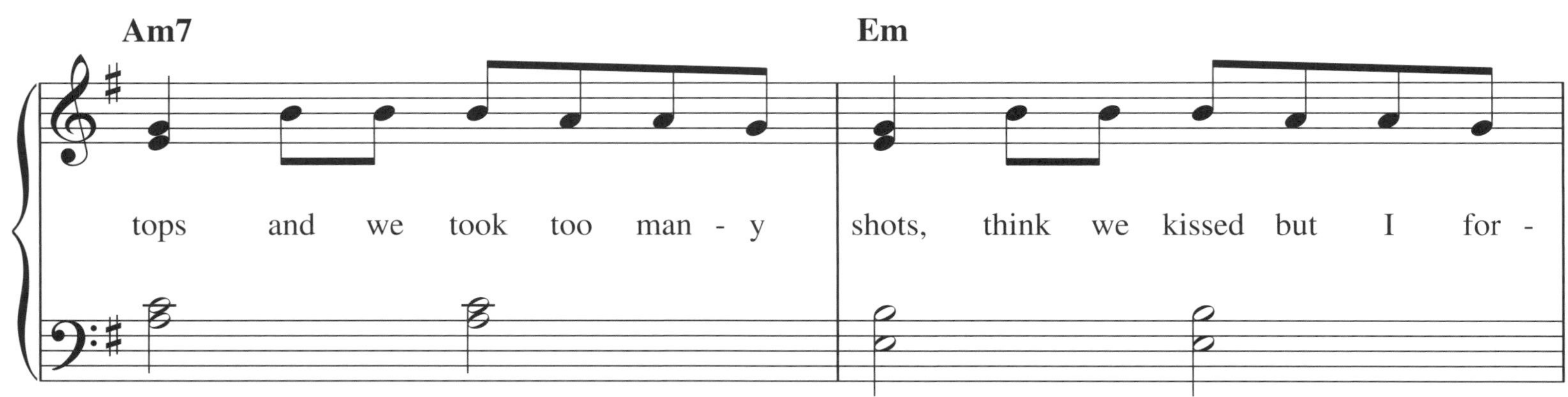
Am7
Em
tops and we took too man - y shots, think we kissed but I for -

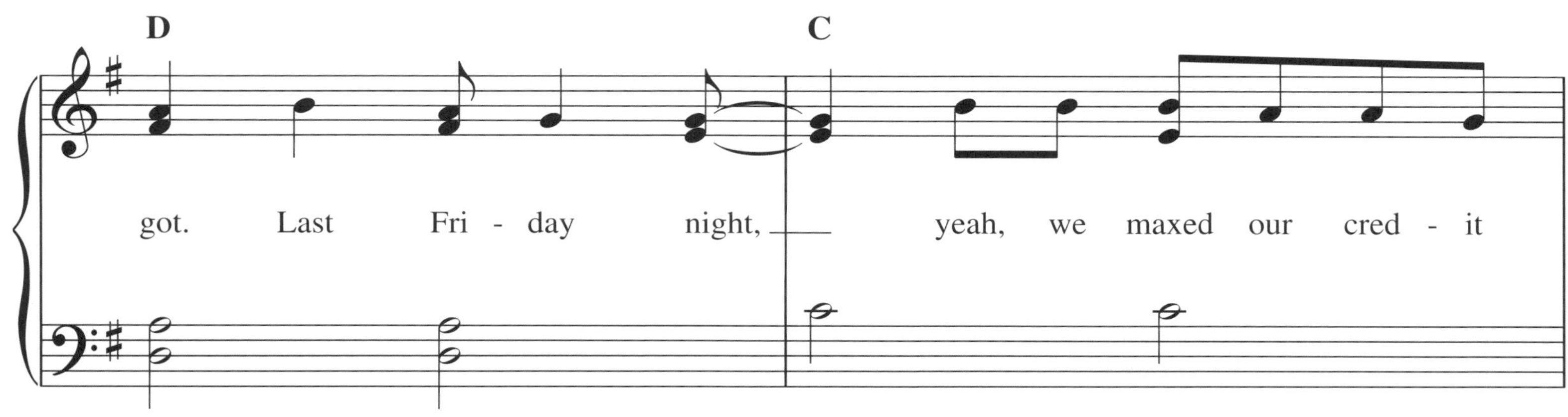
D
C
got. Last Fri - day night, yeah, we maxed our cred - it

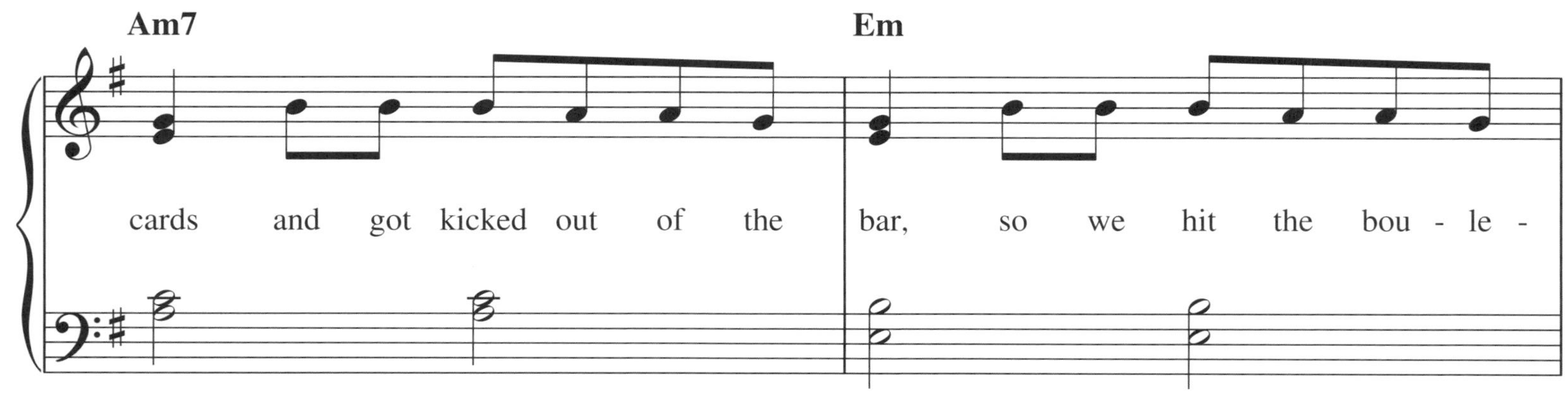
Am7
Em
cards and got kicked out of the bar, so we hit the bou - le -

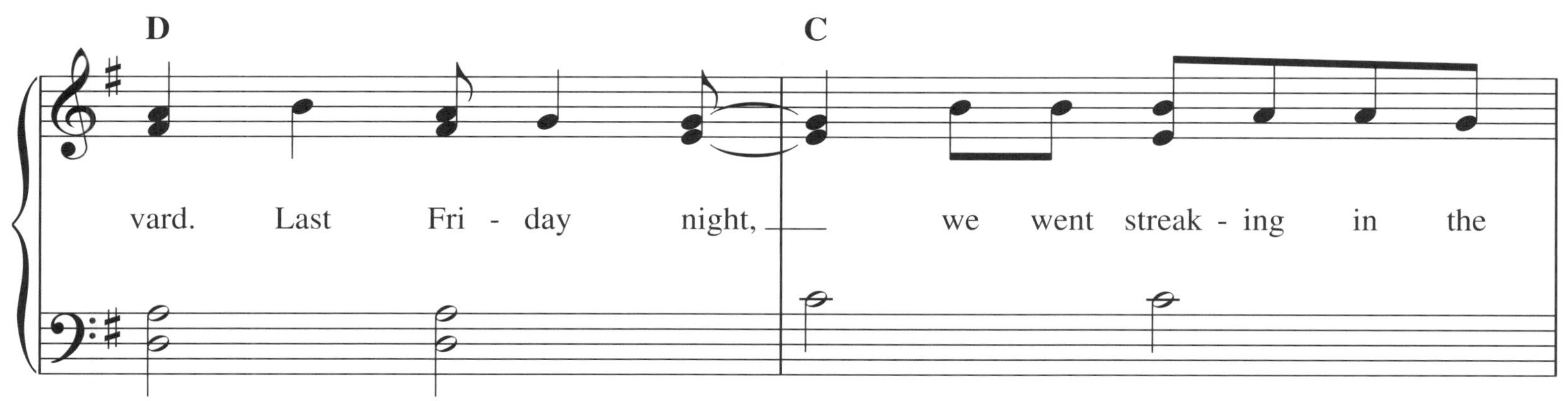
D
C
vard. Last Fri - day night, we went streak - ing in the

Am7
Em
park, skin - ny - dip - ping in the dark, then had a mé - nage à

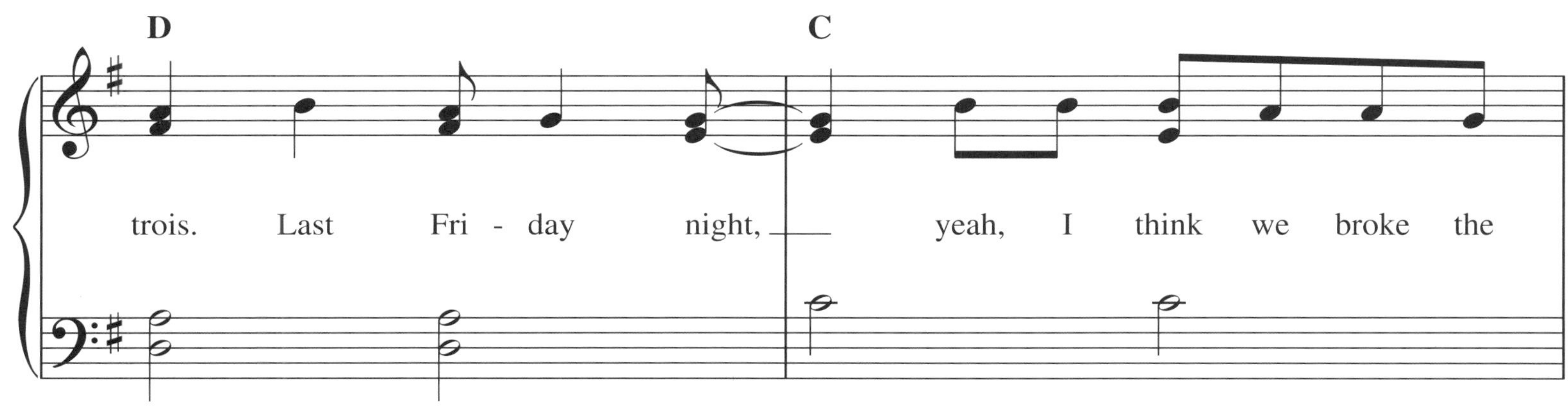
D
C
trois. Last Fri - day night, yeah, I think we broke the

To Coda
Am7
Em
D
law, al-ways say we're gon - na stop - op. Oh, whoa. This Fri-day night,

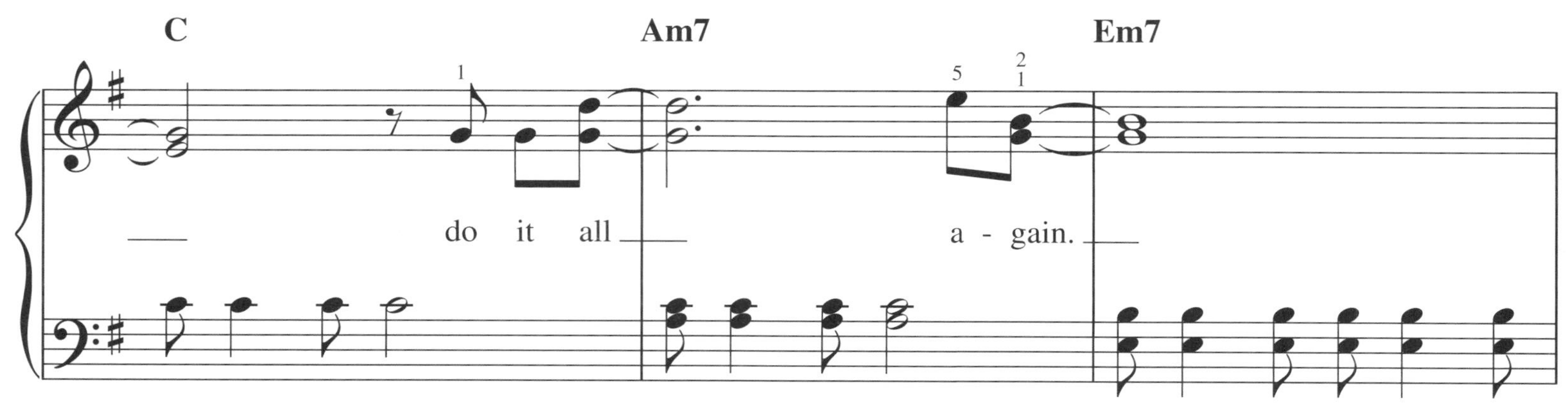
C
Am7
Em7
do it all
a - gain.

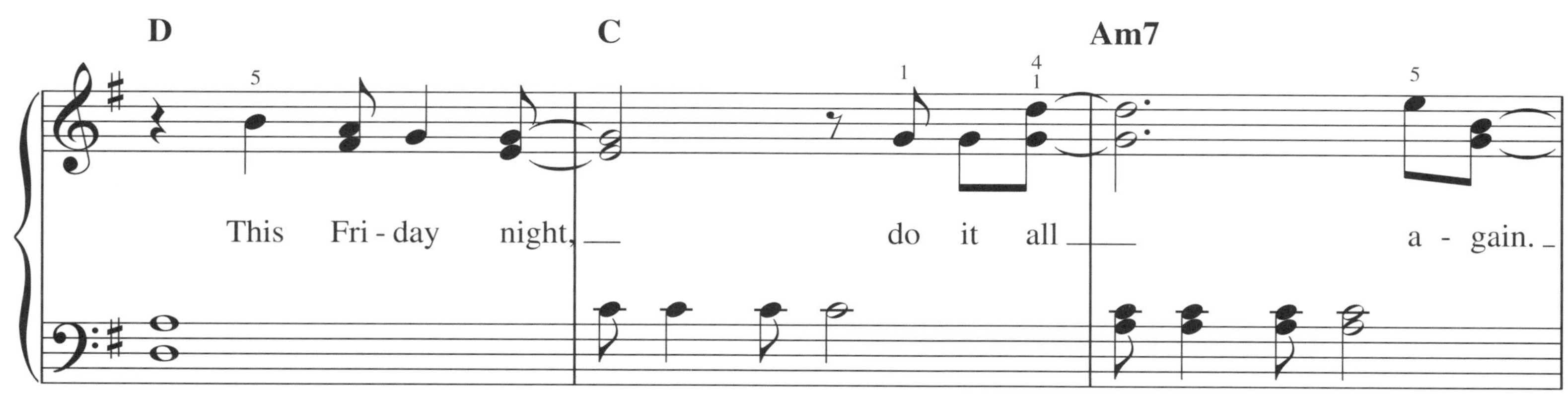
D
C
Am7
This Fri - day night,
do it all
a - gain.

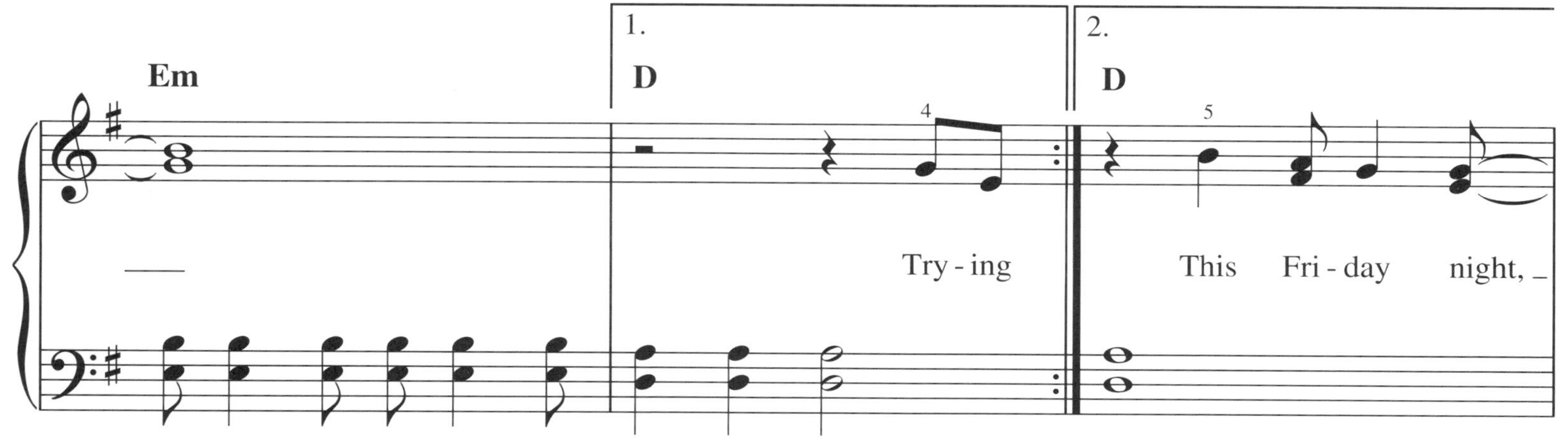
Em
1.
D
2.
D
Try - ing
This Fri - day night,

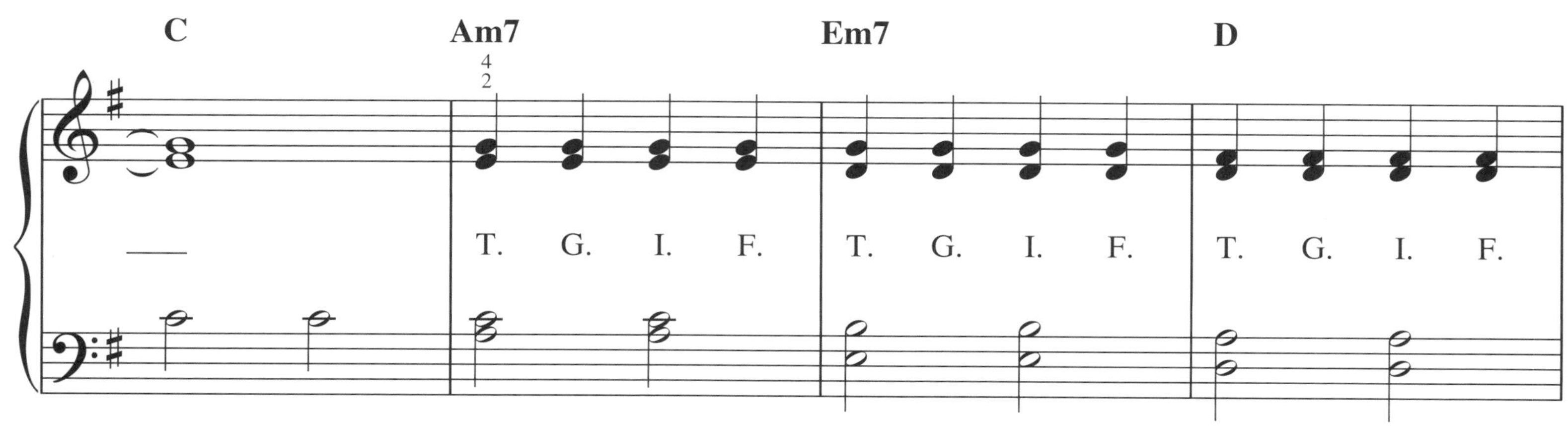
C
Am7
Em7
D
T. G. I. F.
T. G. I. F.
T. G. I. F.

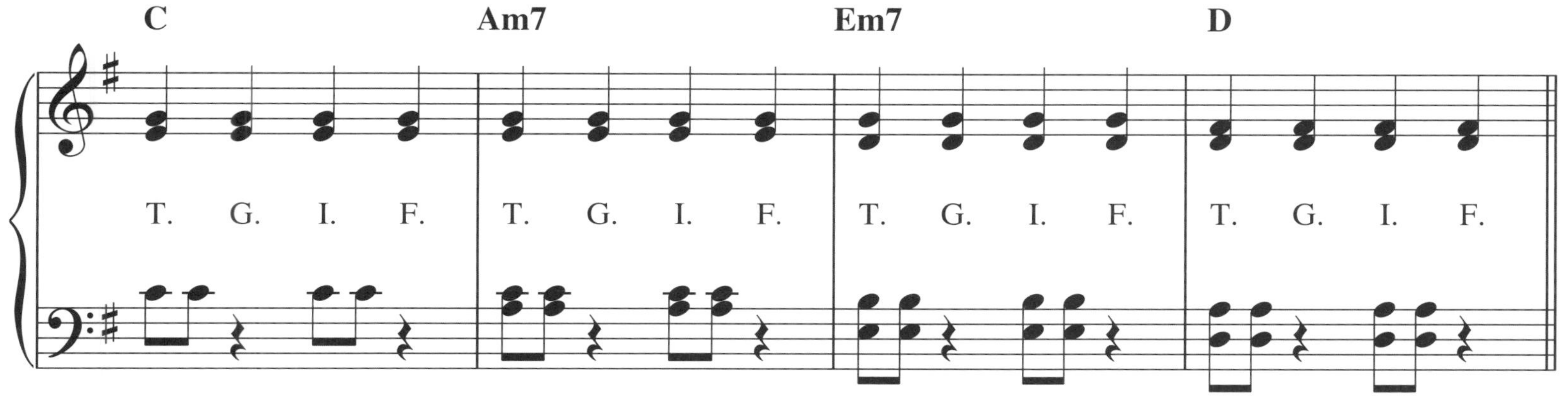
C
Am7
Em7
D
T. G. I. F. T. G. I. F. T. G. I. F. T. G. I. F.

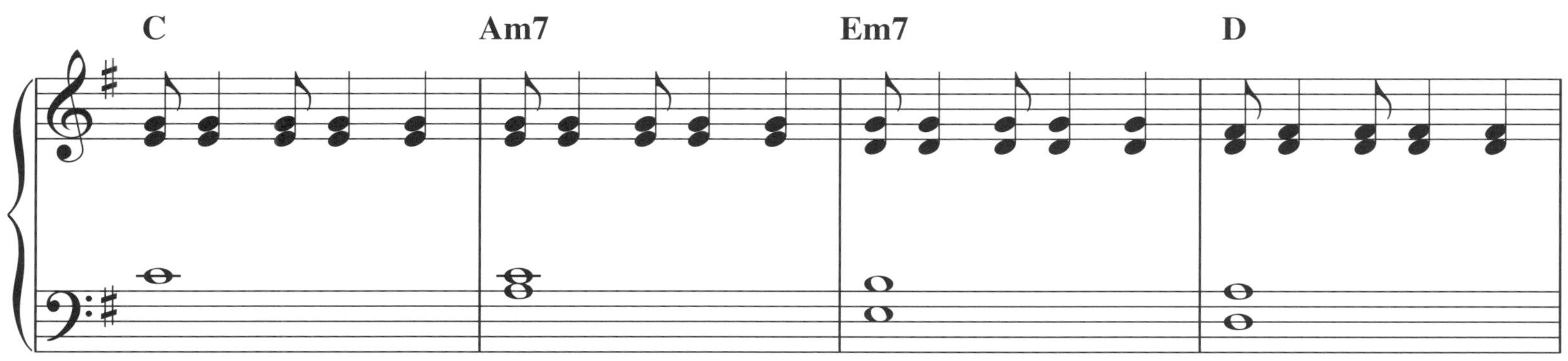
C
Am7
Em7
D

C
Am7
Em7
D.S. al Coda

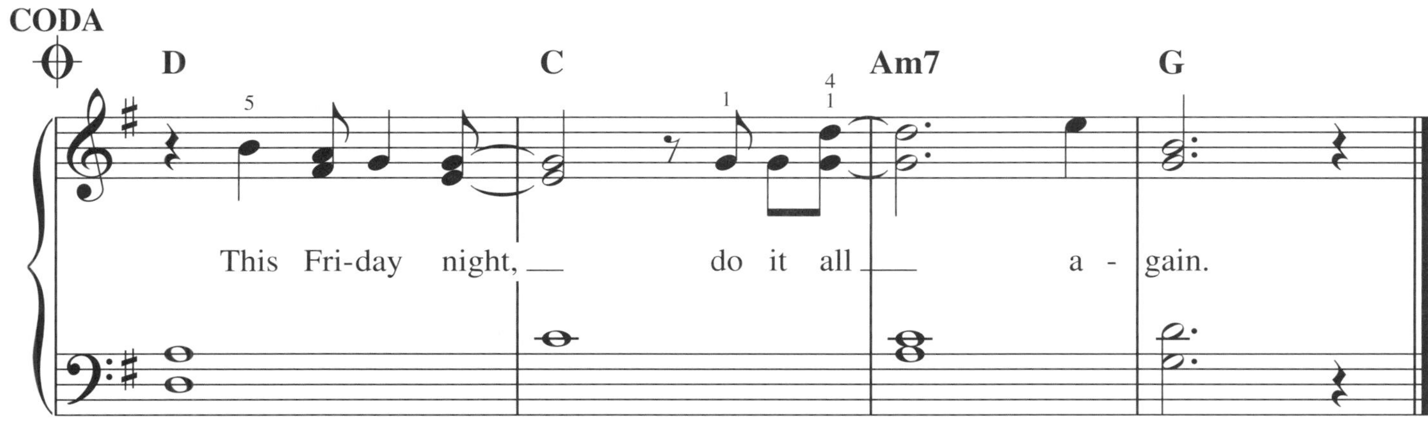
CODA
D
C
Am7
G
This Fri-day night, do it all a - gain.

UPTOWN GIRL

Words and Music by
BILLY JOEL

F
Gm
F/A
up - town girl.
Up - town girl,
She's been liv - ing in her
you know I can't af - ford to
white bread _ world
buy her ___ pearls.

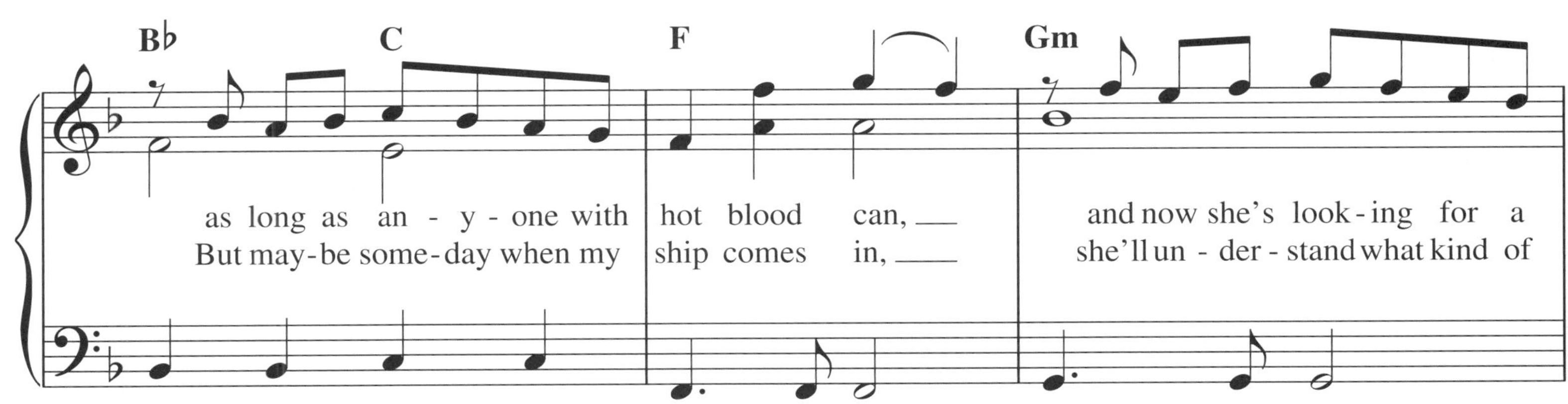
B♭
C
F
Gm
as long as an - y - one with
But may-be some-day when my
hot blood can, ___
ship comes in, ___
and now she's look - ing for a
she'll un - der - stand what kind of

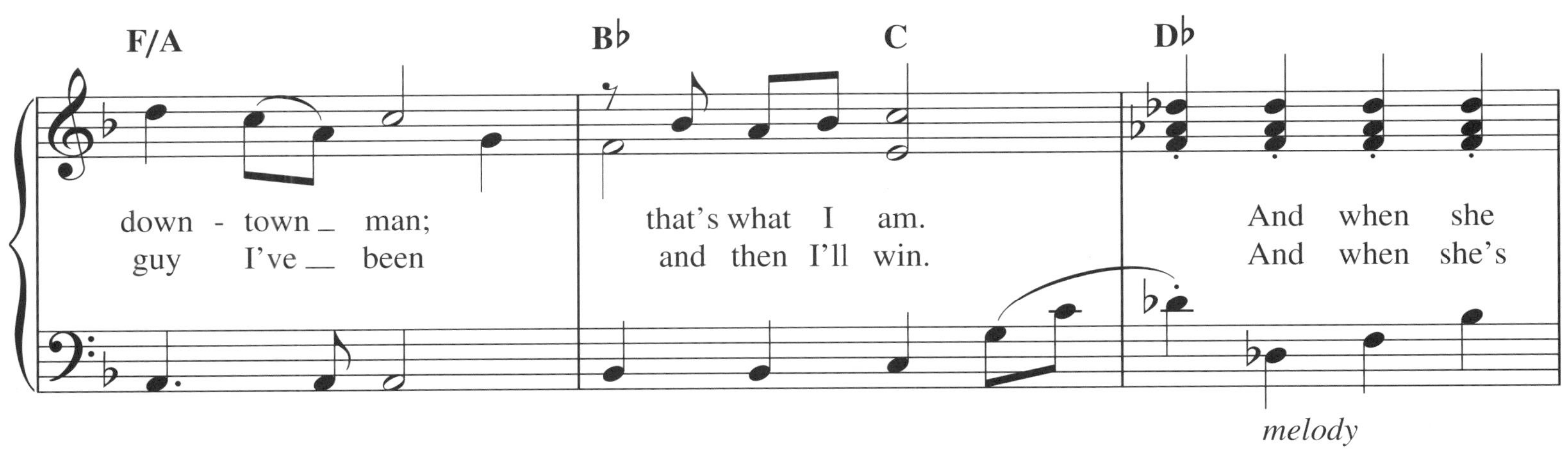
F/A
B♭
C
D♭
down - town _ man;
guy I've __ been
that's what I am.
and then I'll win.
And when she
And when she's
melody

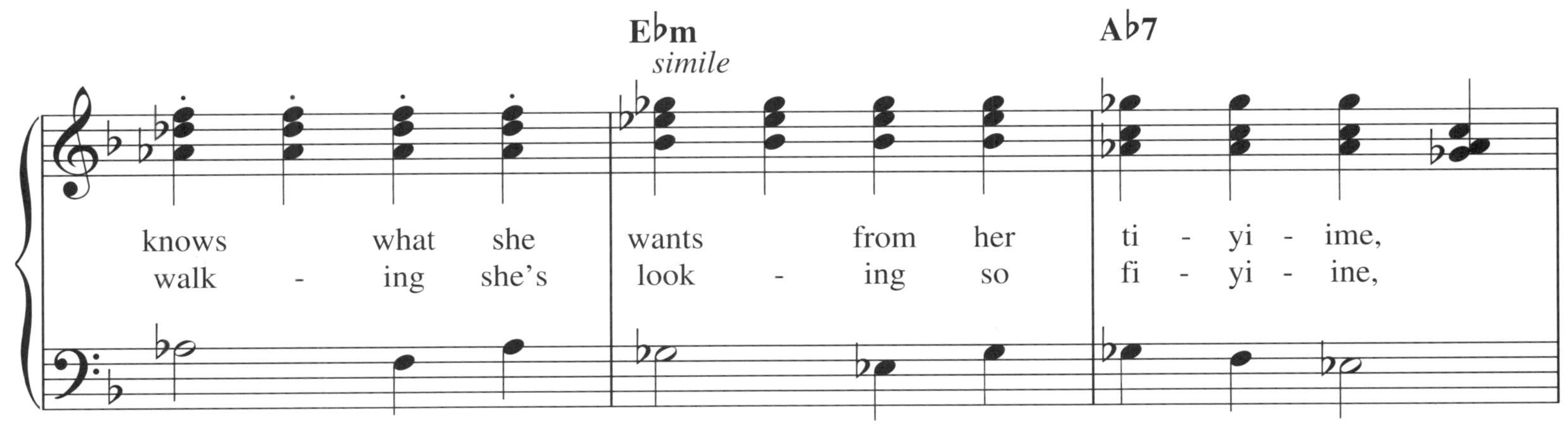
E♭m
simile
A♭7
knows what she
walk - ing she's
wants from her
look - ing so
ti - yi - ime,
fi - yi - ine,

D♭
Cm7♭5
and when she wakes up and makes up her
and when she's talk - ing she'll say that she's

F7♭9
B♭
Gm
Cm
melody
mi - yi - ind, she'll see I'm not so tough just be - cause
mi - yi - ine. She'll say I'm not so tough just be - cause
5

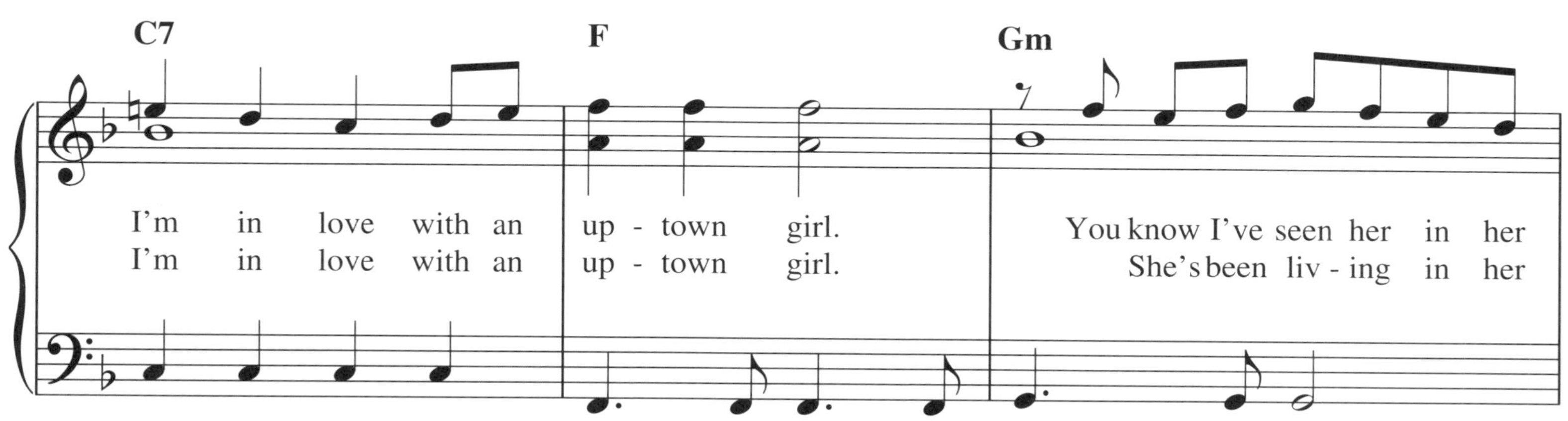
C7
F
Gm
I'm in love with an up - town girl. You know I've seen her in her
I'm in love with an up - town girl. She's been liv - ing in her

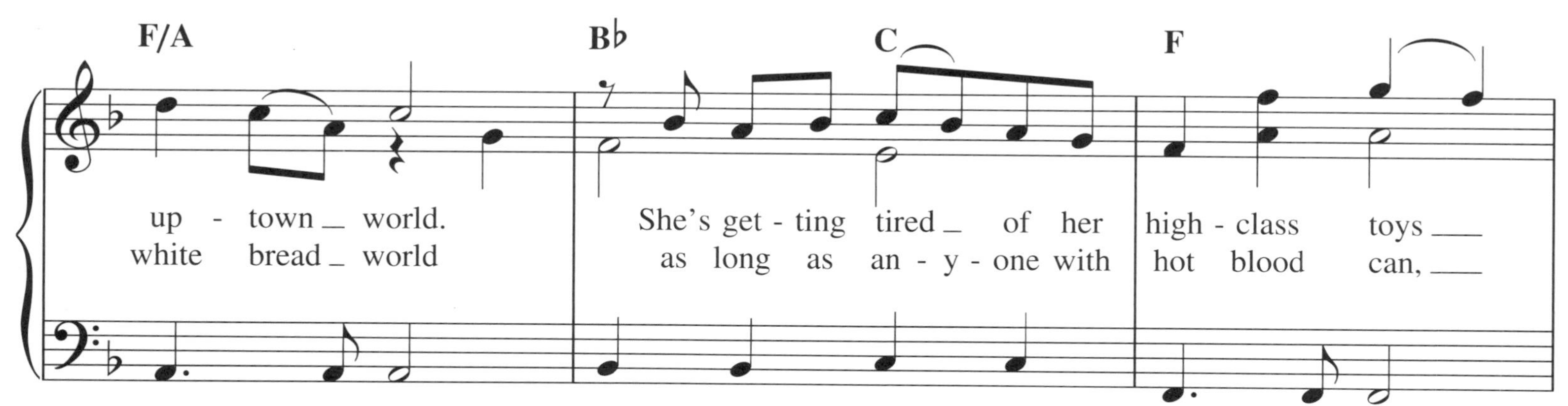
F/A
B♭
C
F
up - town _ world. She's get - ting tired _ of her high - class toys ___
white bread _ world as long as an - y - one with hot blood can, ___

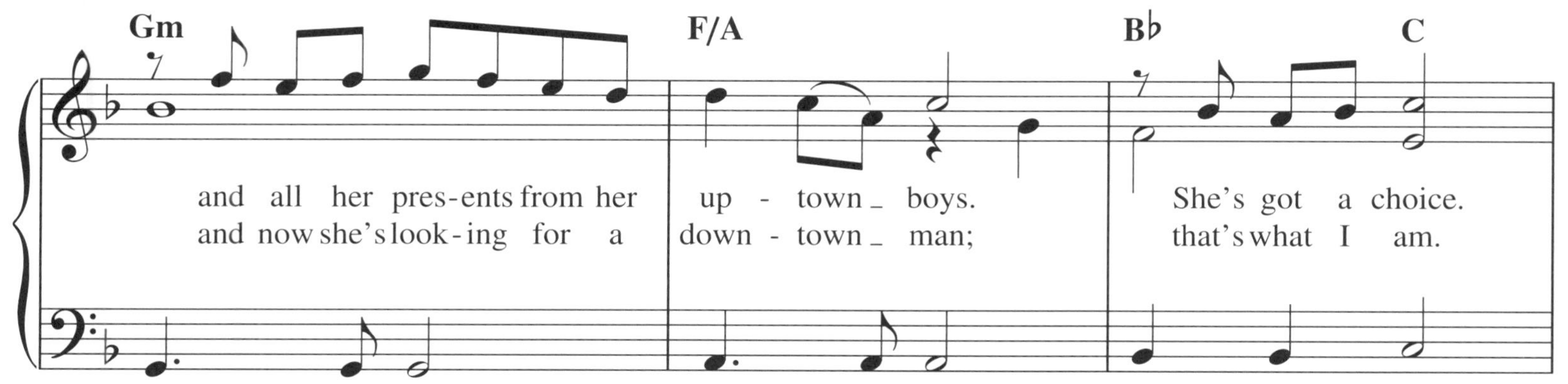
Gm
F/A
B♭
C
and all her pres-ents from her up - town boys.
and now she's look-ing for a down - town man;
She's got a choice.
that's what I am.

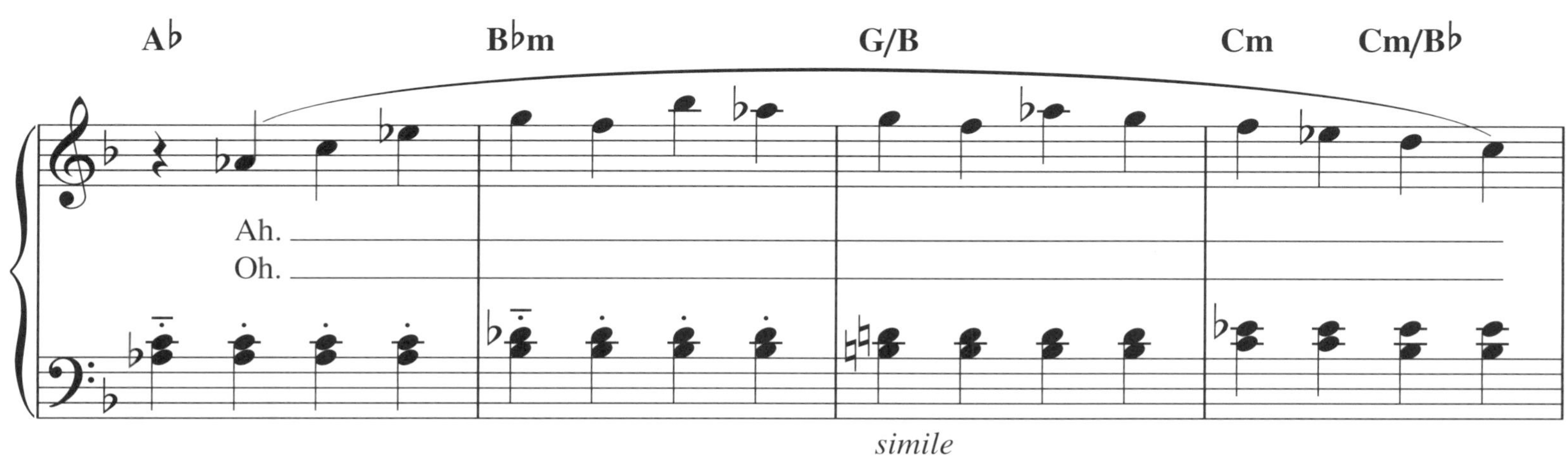
A♭
B♭m
G/B
Cm
Cm/B♭
Ah.
Oh.
simile

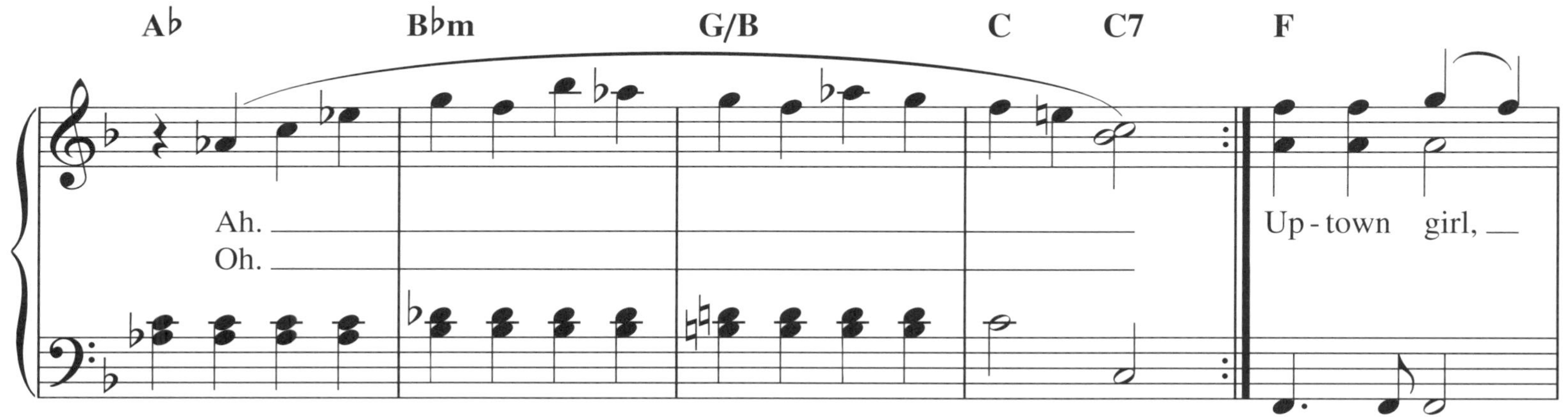
A♭
B♭m
G/B
C
C7
F
Ah.
Oh.
Up-town girl,

Gm
F/A
B♭
C
F
she's my up - town girl. You know I'm in love with an up - town girl.

HOT FOR TEACHER

Words and Music by DAVID LEE ROTH,
EDWARD VAN HALEN, ALEX VAN HALEN
and MICHAEL ANTHONY

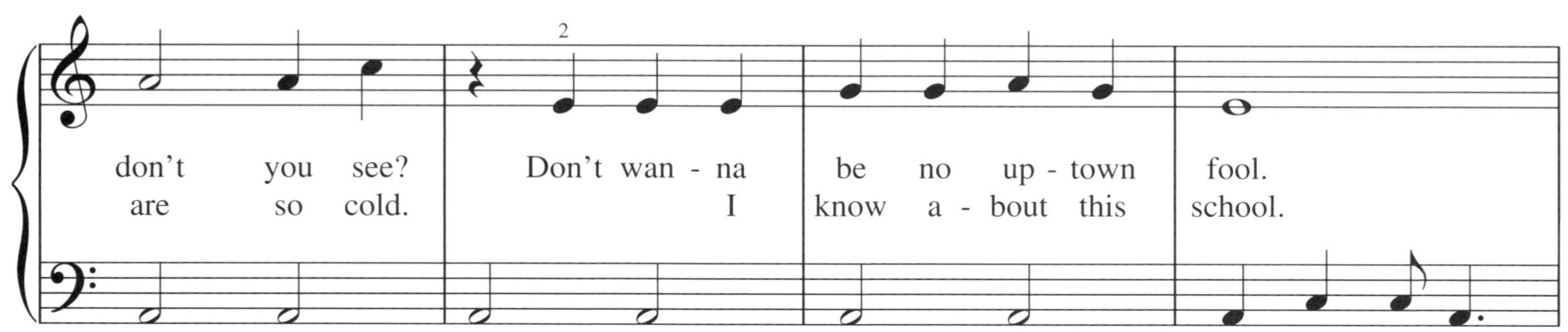

May - be I should go to hell,
Lit - tle girl from Cher - ry Lawn, how
1

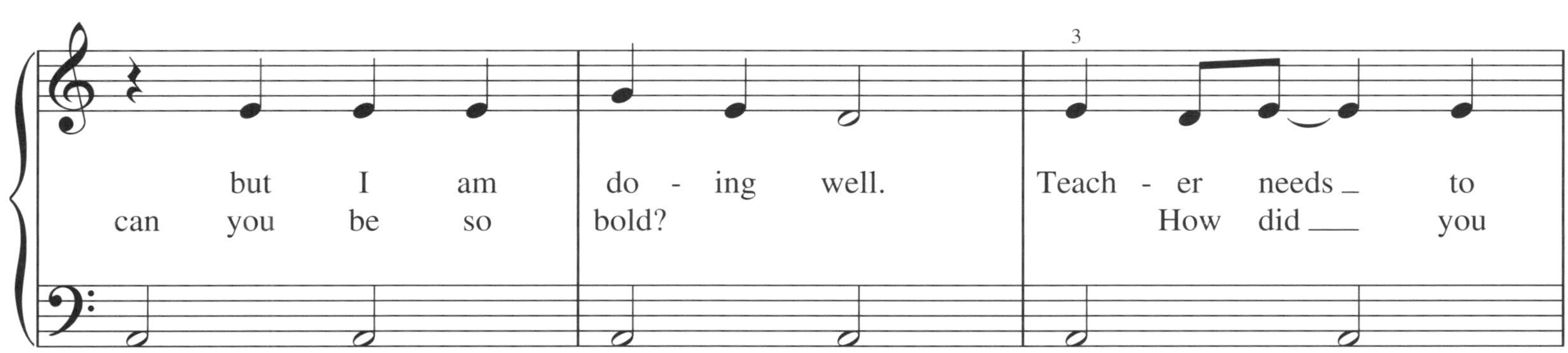
3
but I am do - ing well. Teach - er needs to
can you be so bold? How did you

see me af - ter school.
know that gold - en rule?

D
3
I think of all the ed - u - ca - tion that I've
1
5

G
missed.
But then, my home - work was nev - er quite like

this.

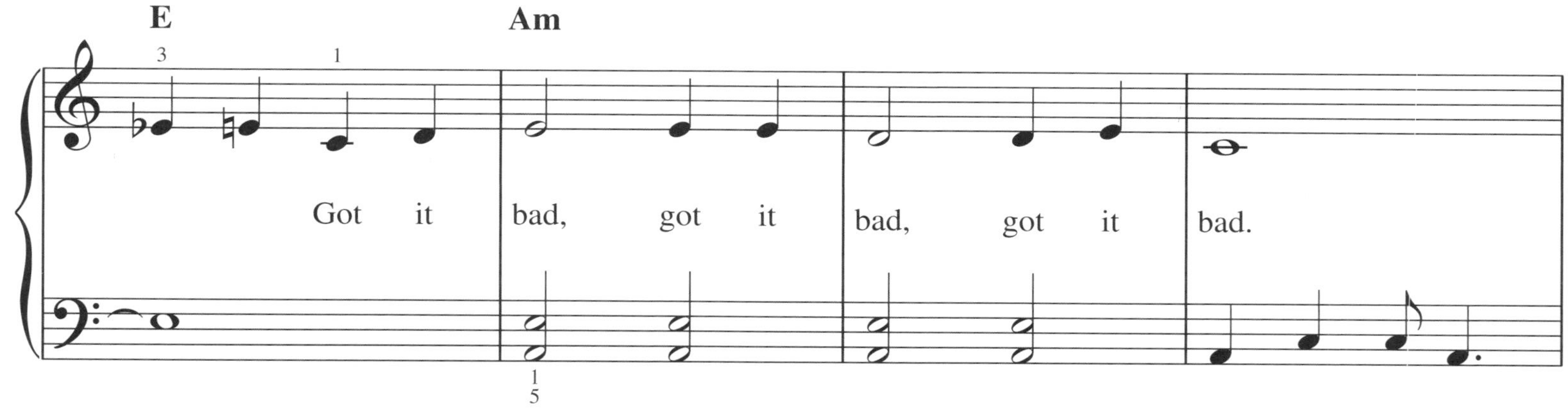
E
Am
Got it bad, got it bad, got it bad.

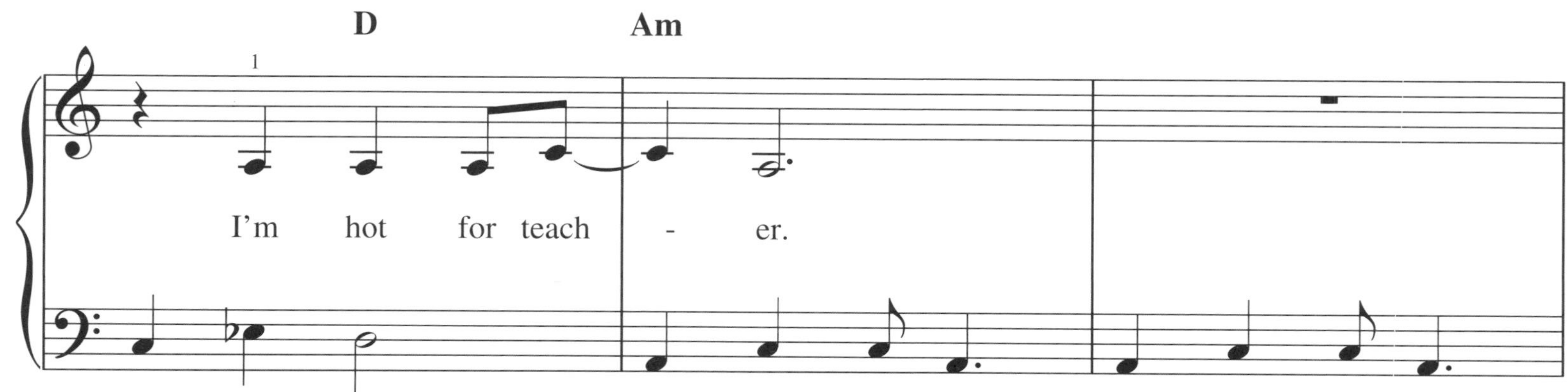
D
Am
I'm hot for teach - er.

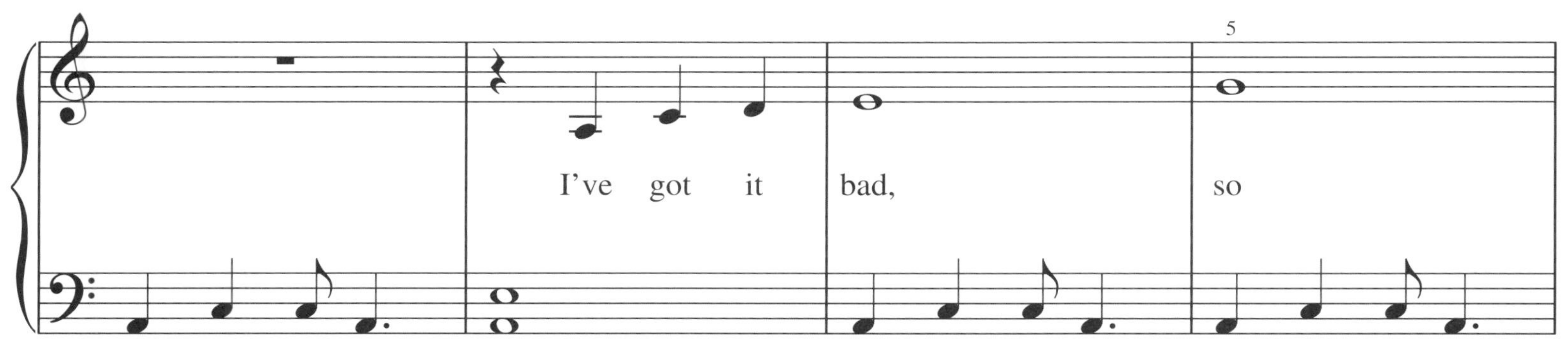
I've got it bad,
so

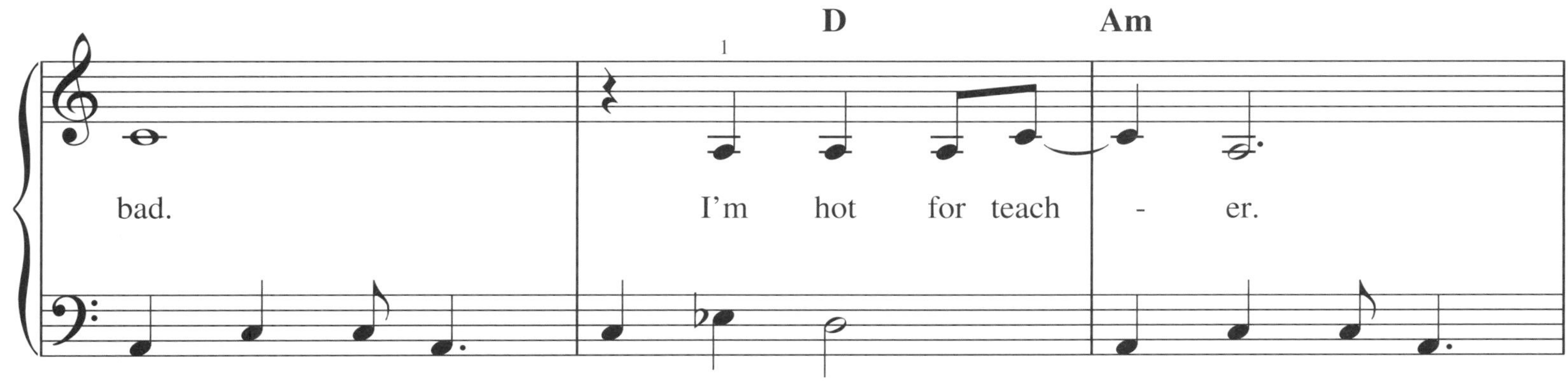
D
Am
bad.
I'm hot for teach - er.

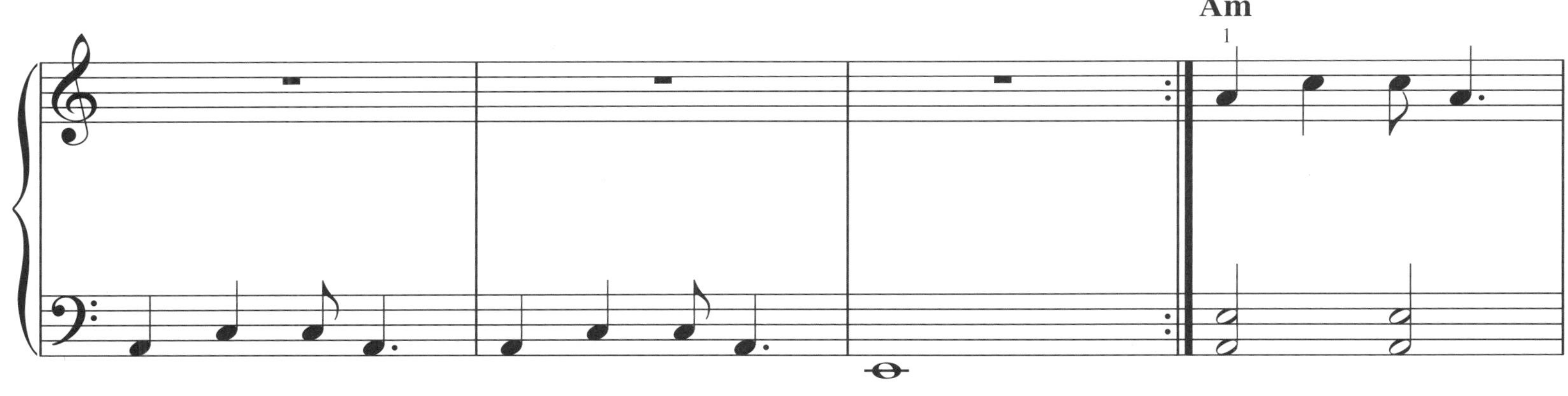
Am

D5

Am

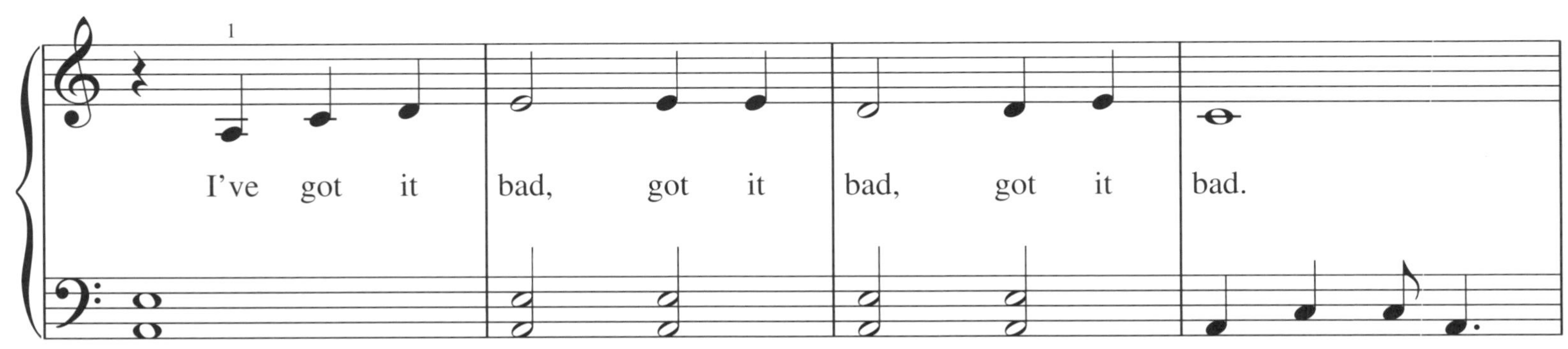
1
I've got it bad, got it bad, got it bad.

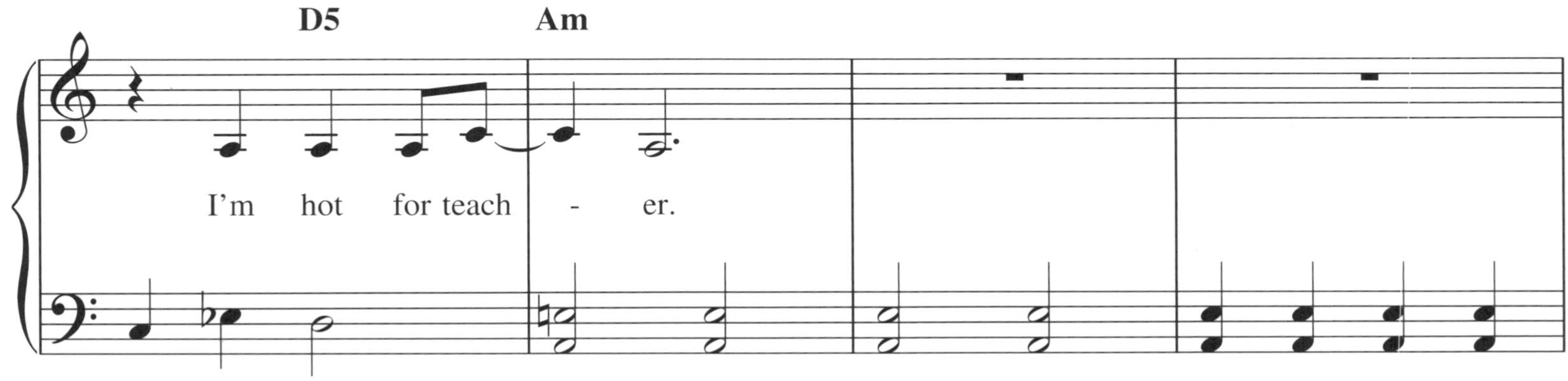
D5
Am
I'm hot for teach - er.

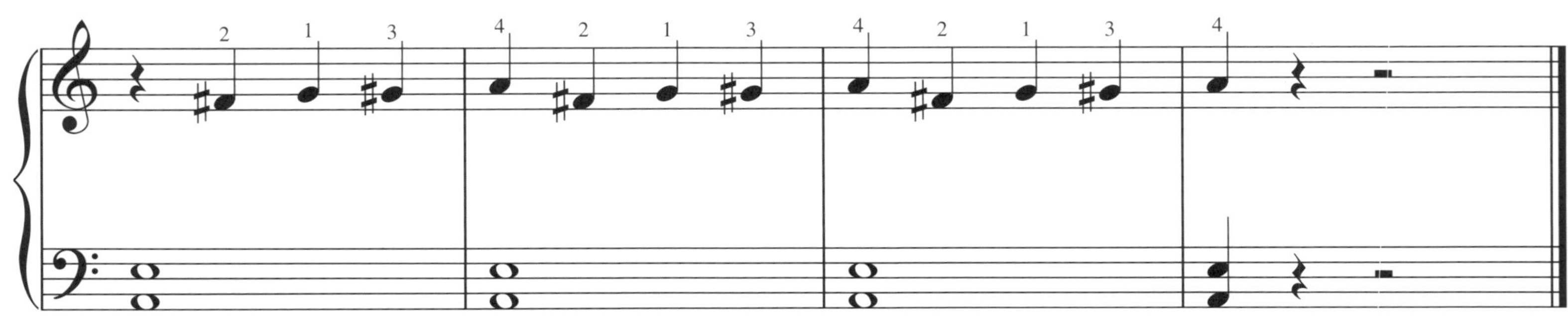
2 1 3 4 2 1 3 4 2 1 3 4

ABC

Words and Music by ALPHONSO MIZELL,
FREDERICK PERREN, DEKE RICHARDS
and BERRY GORDY

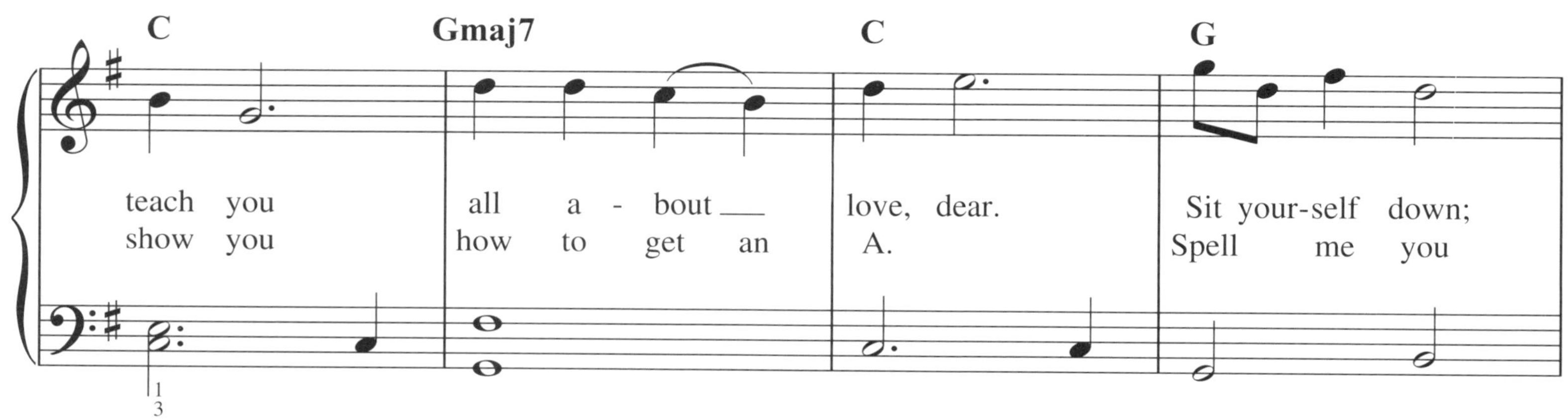
C
Gmaj7
C
G
teach you
all a - bout
love, dear.
Sit your-self down;
show you
how to get an
A.
Spell me you

C
G
C
take a seat;
all you got - ta do is re -
peat af - ter me:
add the two,
lis - ten to ba - by, that's
all you got - ta do.

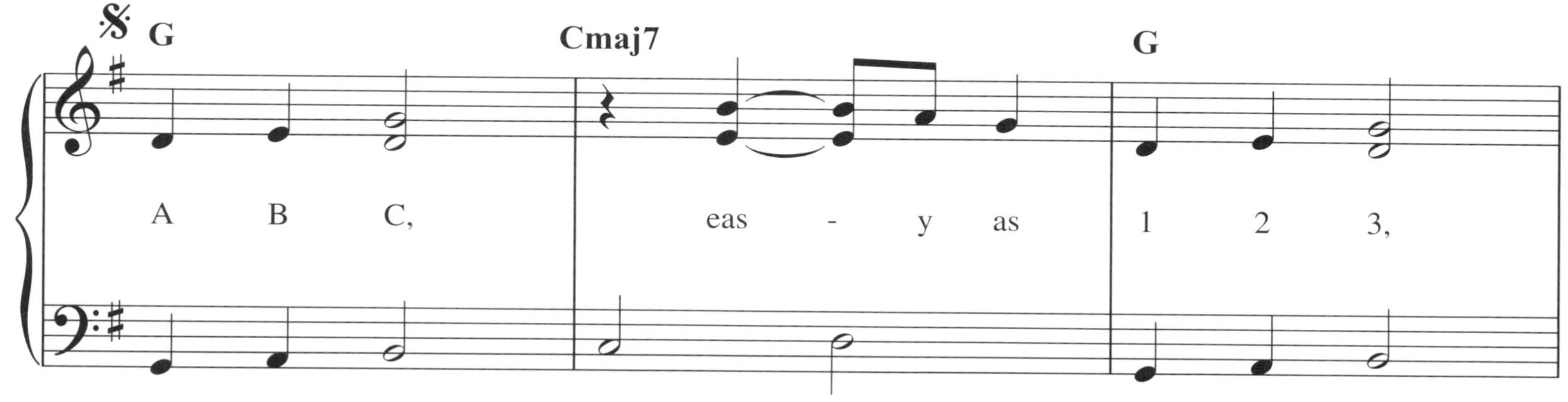
G
Cmaj7
G
A B C,
eas - y as
1 2 3,

Cmaj7
G
C
ah, sim - ple as
do, re, mi,
A B C,

G
C
G
1 2 3, ba - by,
you and me, girl.
A B C,

Cmaj7
G
Cmaj7
eas - y as
1 2 3,
ah, sim - ple as

G
C
G
do re mi,
A B C,
1 2 3, (ba - by)

C
1.
you and me, girl.

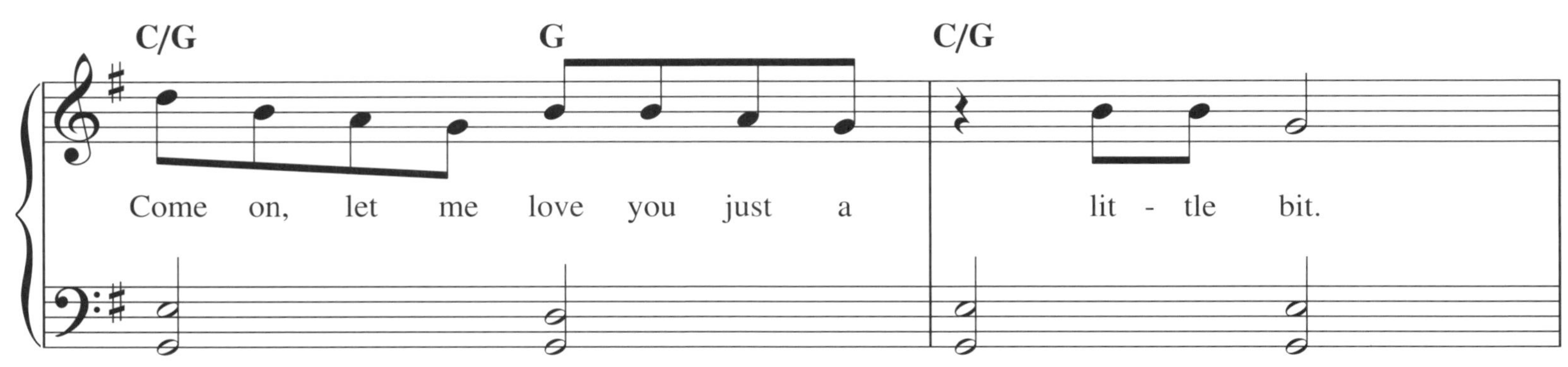
C/G
G
C/G
Come on, let me love you just a
lit - tle bit.

G
C/G
G
I'm gon - na teach you how to
sing it out.

C/G
Com - a, com - a, come on let me
show you what it's all a - bout.

2.
N.C.
Yah,

3
sit down, girl.
I think I love you.

No, get up, girl.
Show me what you can do.

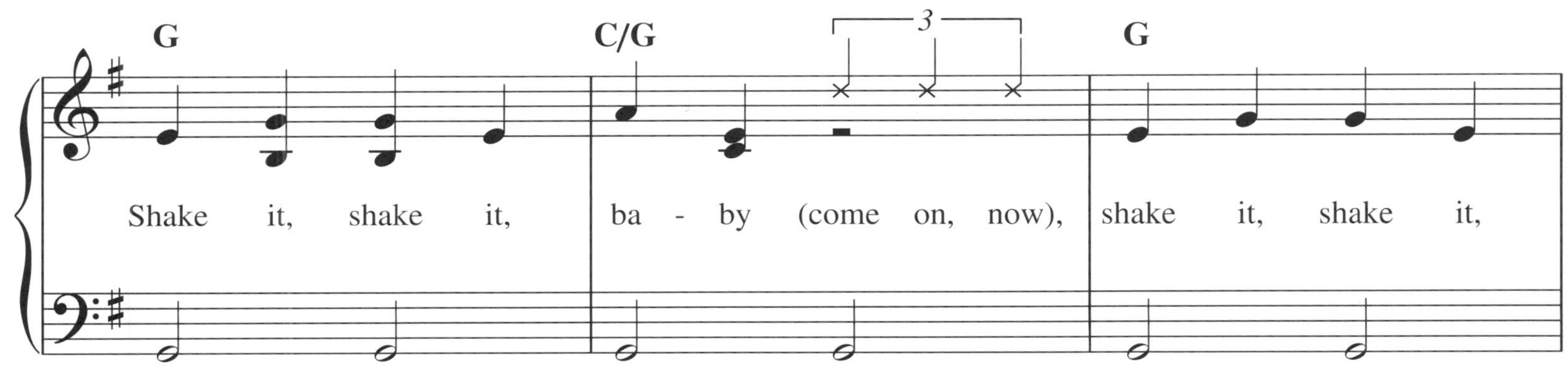
G
C/G
3
G
Shake it, shake it, ba - by (come on, now), shake it, shake it,

D.S. and Fade
C/G
G
C/G
ba - by, oo, shake it, shake it, ba - by (hey).

RUMOUR HAS IT/ SOMEONE LIKE YOU

RUMOUR HAS IT
Words and Music by ADELE ADKINS
and RYAN TEDDER

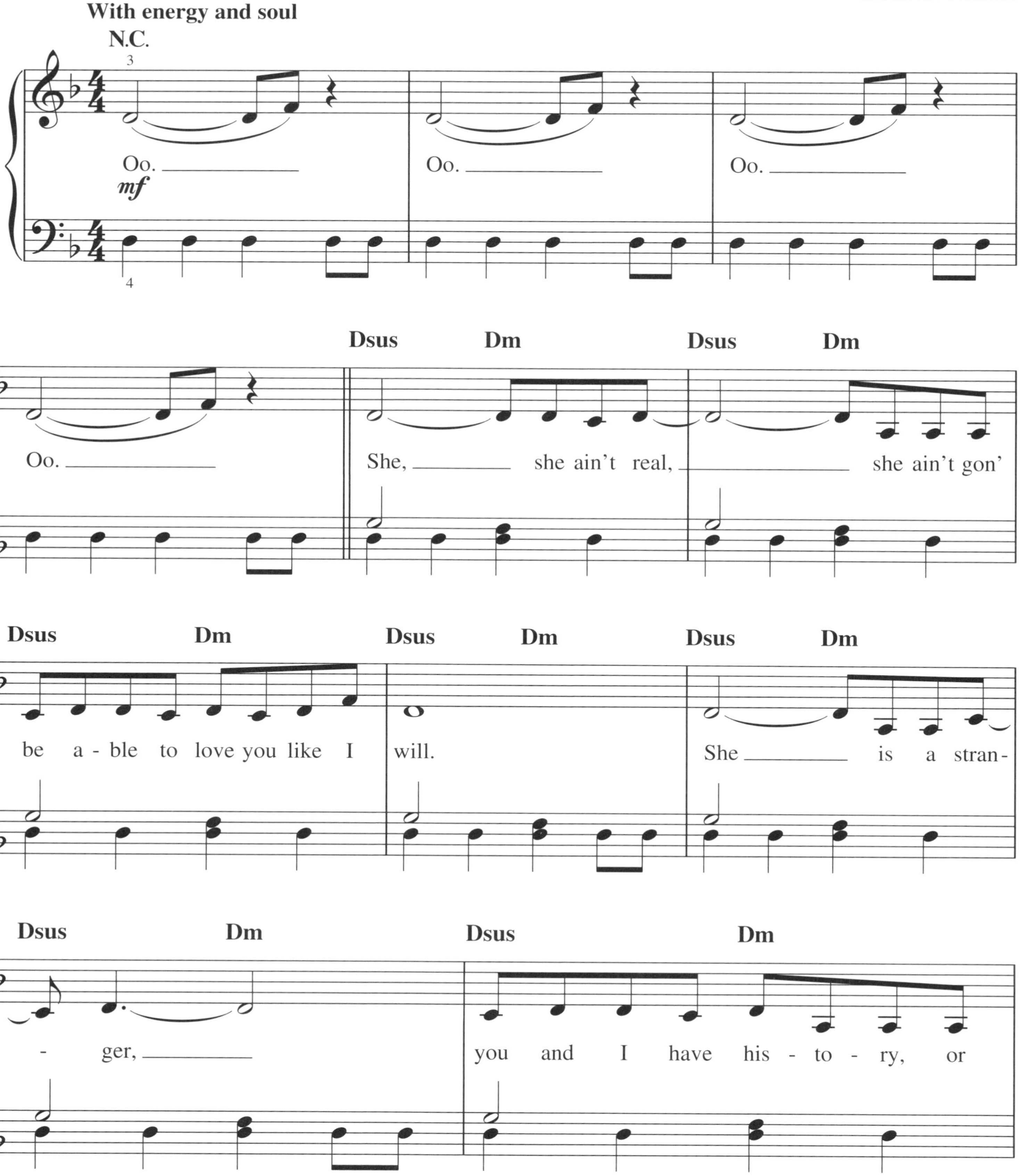
With energy and soul
N.C.
mf
Oo.
Oo.
Oo.
Oo.
Dsus Dm Dsus Dm
She, she ain't real, she ain't gon'
Dsus Dm Dsus Dm Dsus Dm
be a - ble to love you like I will.
She is a stran -
Dsus Dm Dsus Dm
- ger, you and I have his - to - ry, or

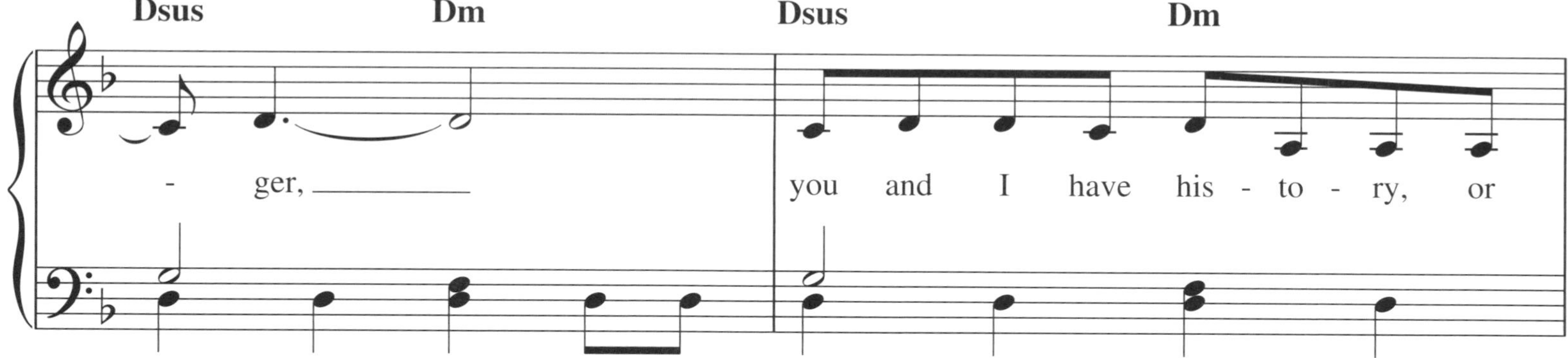

Dsus
Dm
Dsus
Dm
Dsus
Dm
don't you re - mem - ber? Sure, she's got it all, but

D5
ba - by, is that real - ly what you want?

Dm
Bless your soul, you've got your head in the clouds. You made a

Gm7
fool out of you, and boy, she's bring - ing you down. She made your

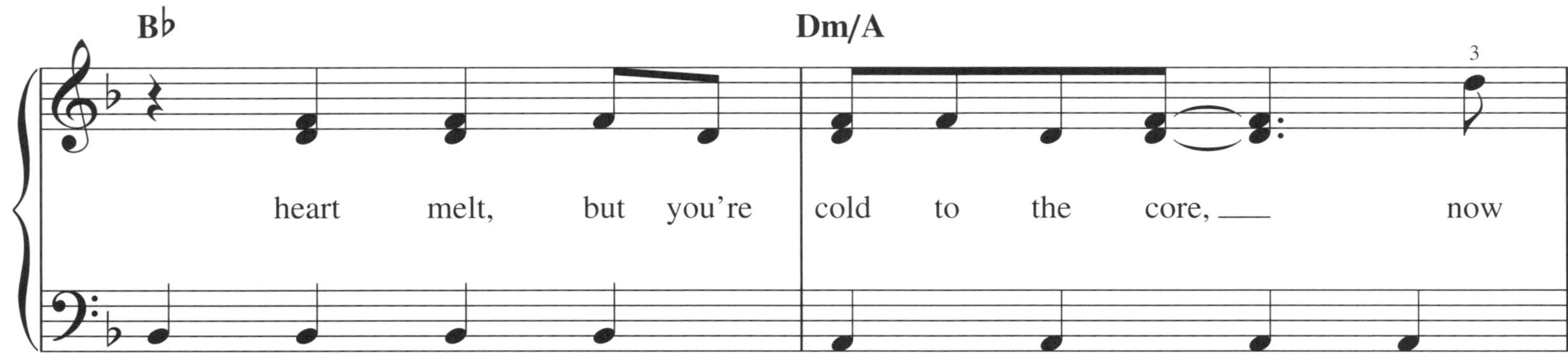
B♭
Dm/A
3
heart melt, but you're cold to the core, now

Gm7
ru - mour has it she ain't got your love an - y - more. Ru - mour has it.

Dm
Ru - mour has it.
Ru - mour has it.

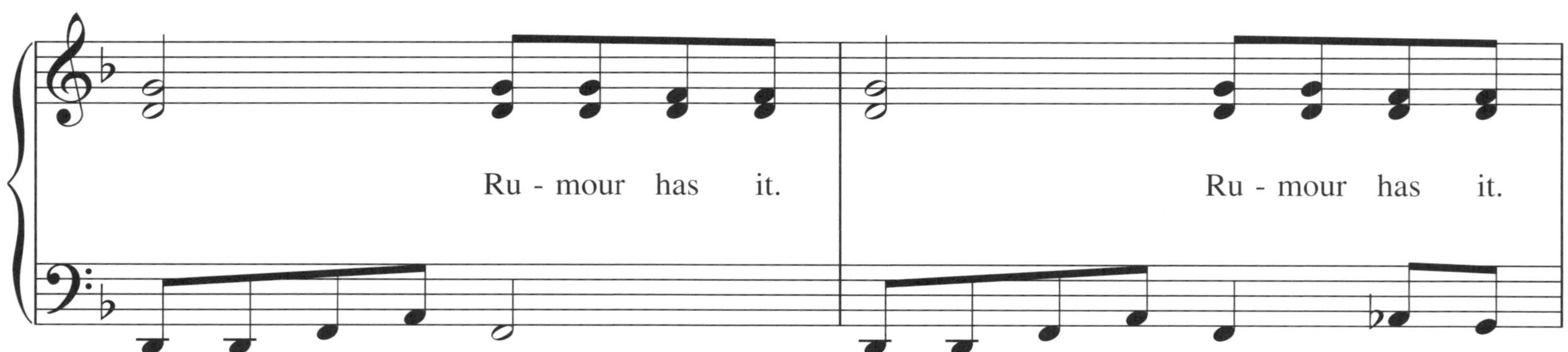
Ru - mour has it.
Ru - mour has it.

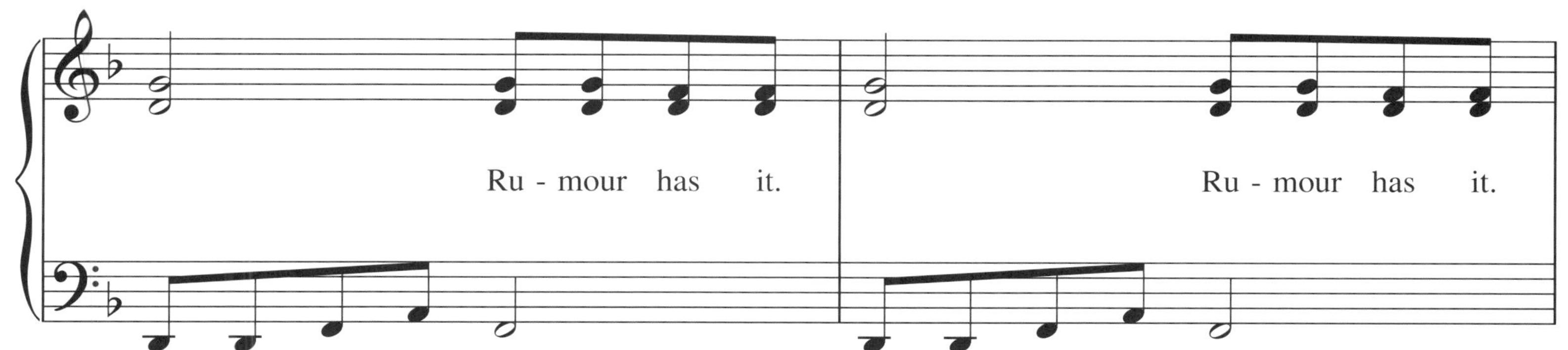

SOMEONE LIKE YOU
Words and Music by ADELE ADKINS
and DAN WILSON

Ballad Tempo

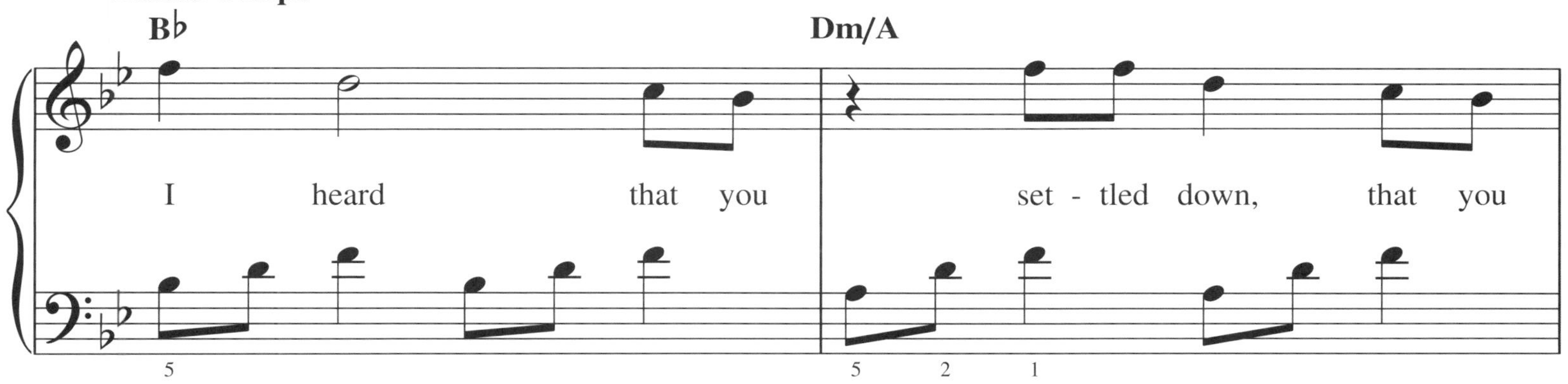

B♭
Dm/A
5
4
I heard that your dreams came true. Guess she

Gm/D
E♭/G
gave you things I did-n't give to you.
accel.

Tempo I
Dm
Ru - mour has it.
Ru - mour has it.

Ru - mour has it.
Ru - mour has it.

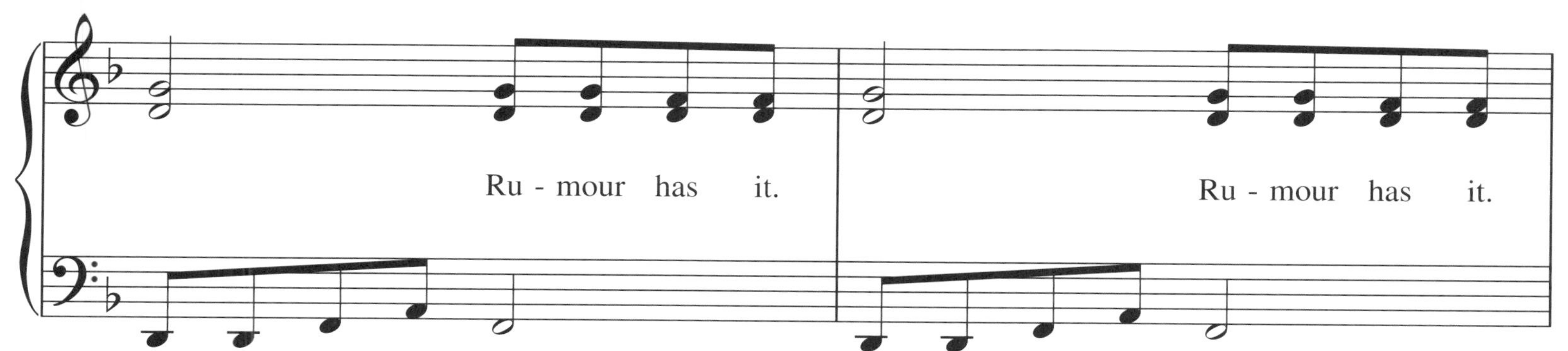

Ru - mour has it.
Ru - mour has it.

To Coda
Ru - mour has it.
Ru - mour.

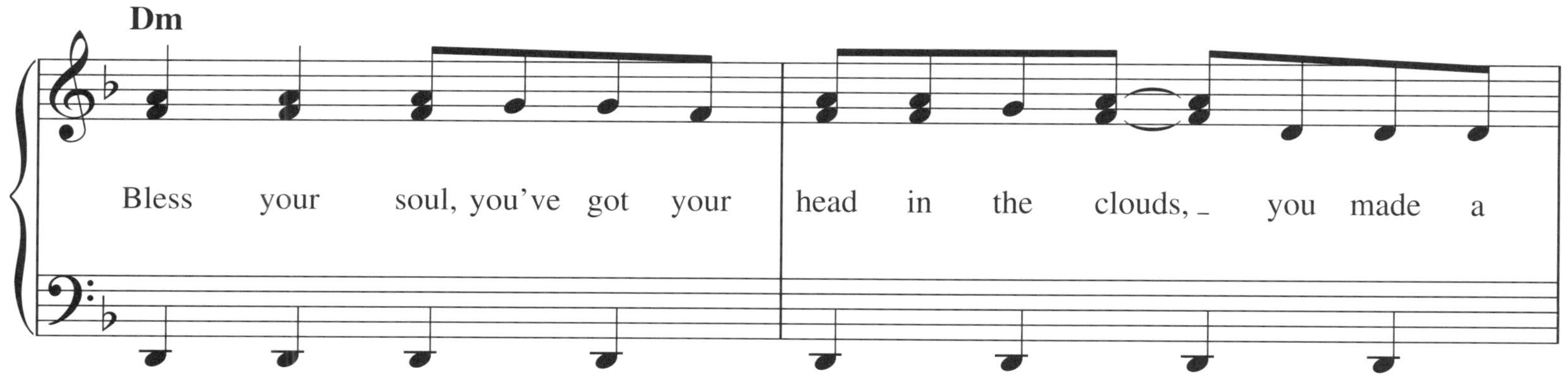

Dm
Bless your soul, you've got your head in the clouds, you made a

Gm7
fool out of me and boy, you're bring - ing me down. You made my

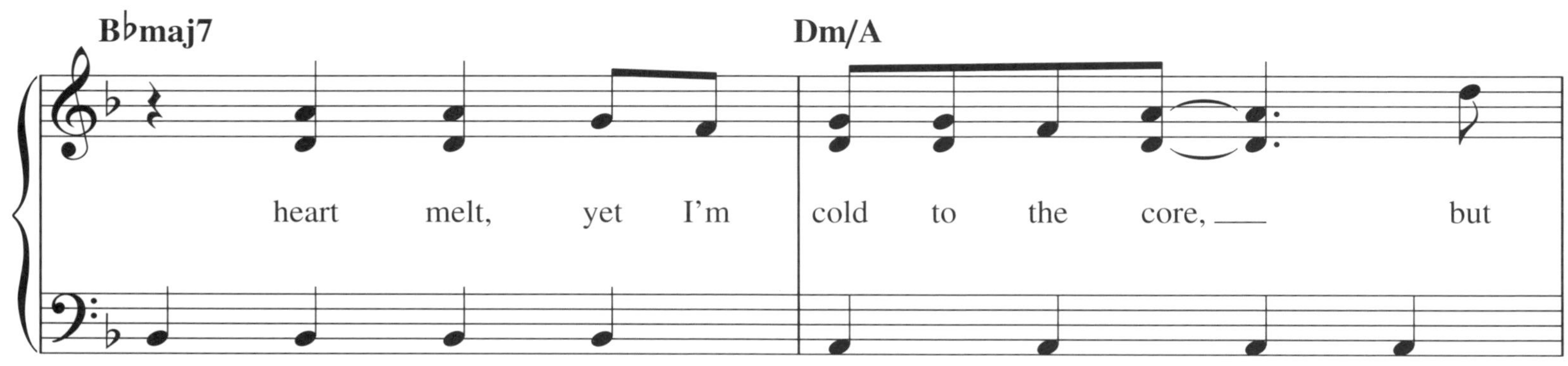
B♭maj7
Dm/A
heart melt, yet I'm cold to the core, ___ but

Gm7
D.S. al Coda
ru - mour has it I'm the one you're leav - ing her for. Ru - mour has it.

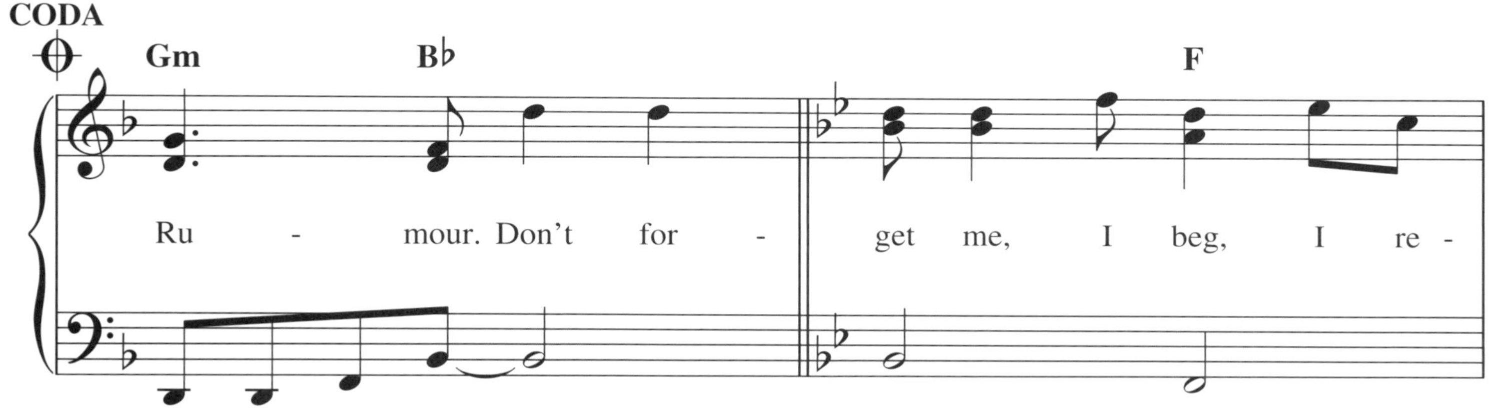
CODA
Gm
B♭
F
Ru - mour. Don't for - get me, I beg, I re -

Gm
E♭
B♭
F
3
mem - ber you said... Nev - er mind, _ I'll find some-one like

Gm
E♭
B♭
F
Gm
E♭
you. I wish noth-ing but the best for you, too. Don't for -

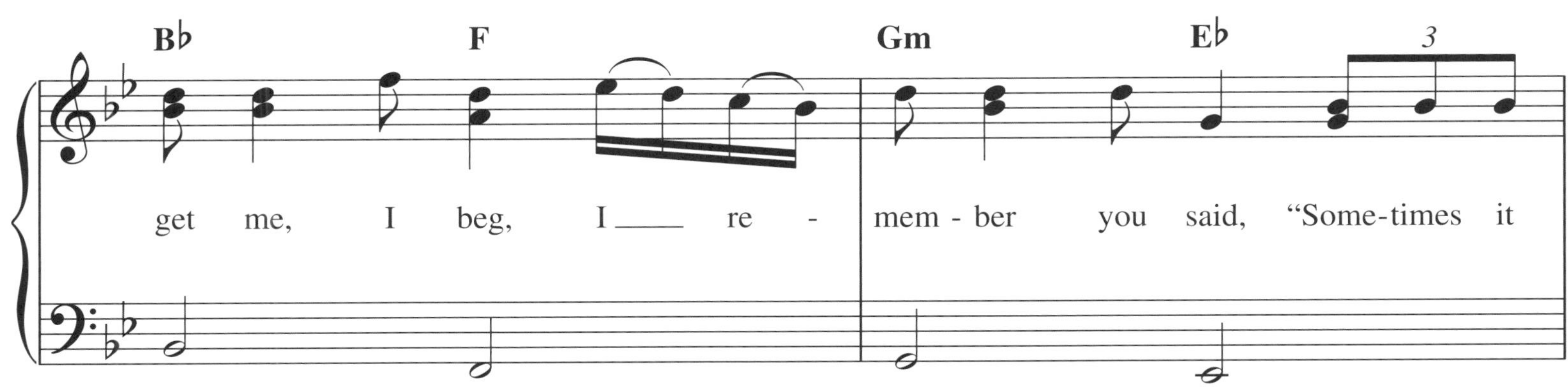
B♭
F
Gm
E♭
3
get me, I beg, I re - mem - ber you said, "Some-times it

B♭
F
3
Gm
E♭
3
lasts in love, but some-times it hurts in - stead." Some-times it

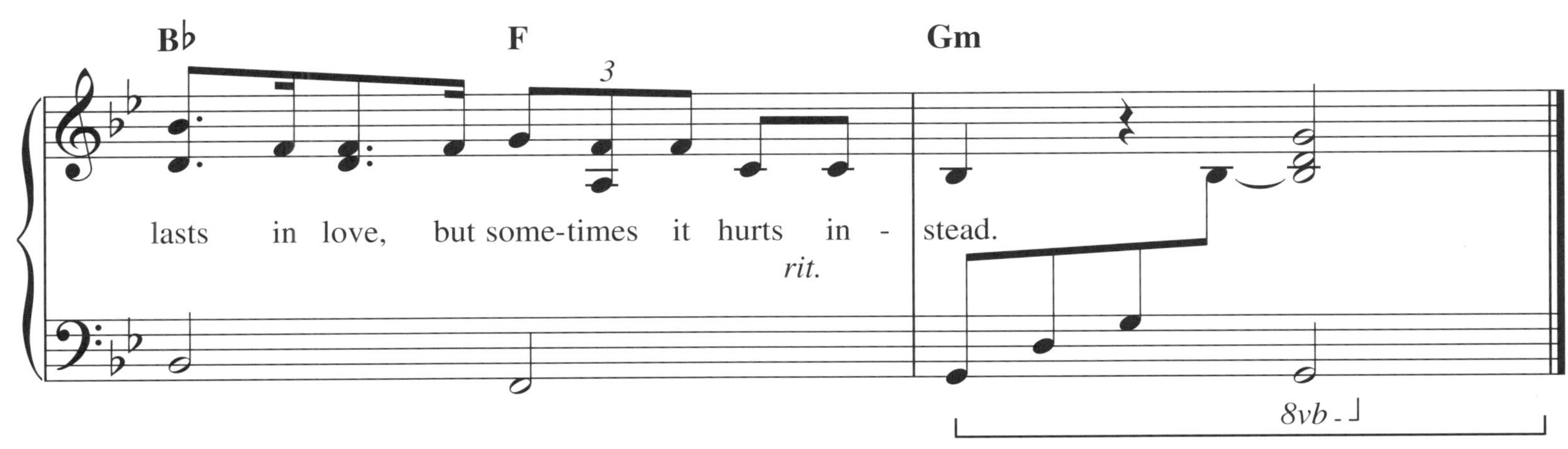
B♭
F
3
Gm
lasts in love, but some-times it hurts in - stead.
rit.
8vb

GIRLS JUST WANT TO HAVE FUN

Words and Music by
ROBERT HAZARD

Em
D
C
1.
Em
D
girls,
girls,
girls,
they want to have fu - un.
Oh,
girls just want to have
G
fun.
Em
C
D
2., 3.
Em
D
G
girls just want to have...
That's all they real - ly want:
Em
some fun.

G
Em
D
When the work - ing day is done, oh, girls, they want to have fu -

C
Em
D
G
un. Oh, girls just want to have fun.

D.S. al Coda
(take 2nd ending)
Em
To Coda
C
D

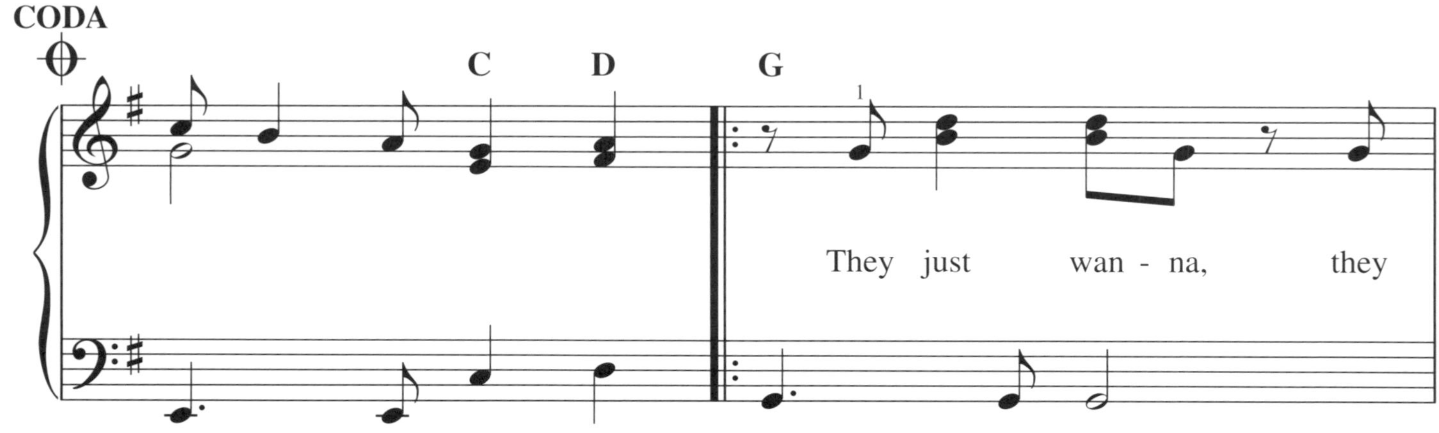
CODA
C
D
G
They just wan - na, they

Em C D G
just wan - na.
They just wan - na, they

Em C D G Em C D
just wan- na.
Girls,
girls just want to have fu -

G
1.
Em C D
2.
Em C D
un.
Girls just want to have fu -

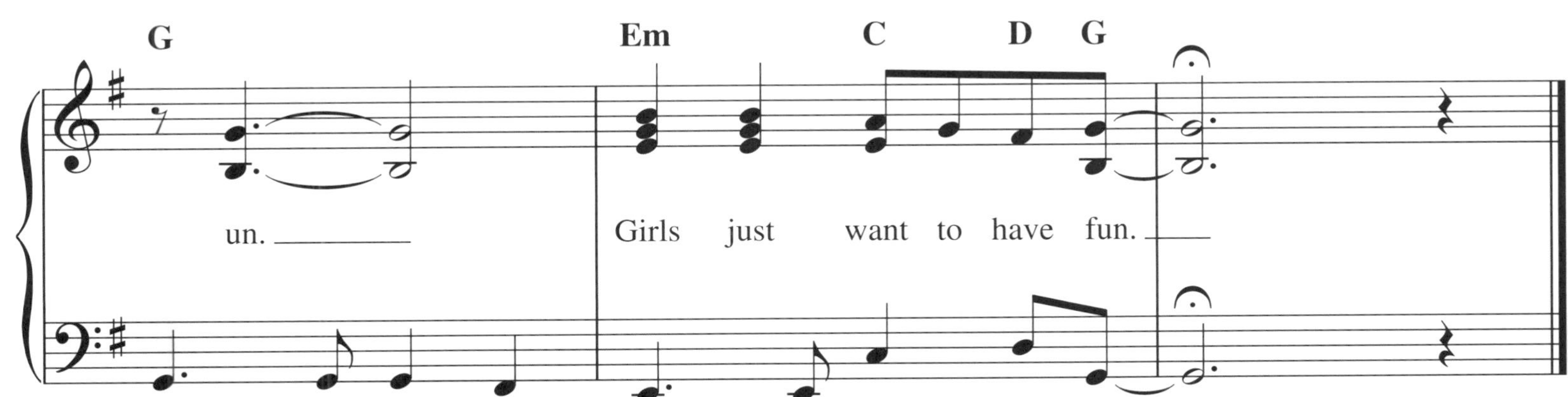
G Em C D G
un.
Girls just want to have fun.

CONSTANT CRAVING

Words and Music by K.D. LANG
and BEN MINK

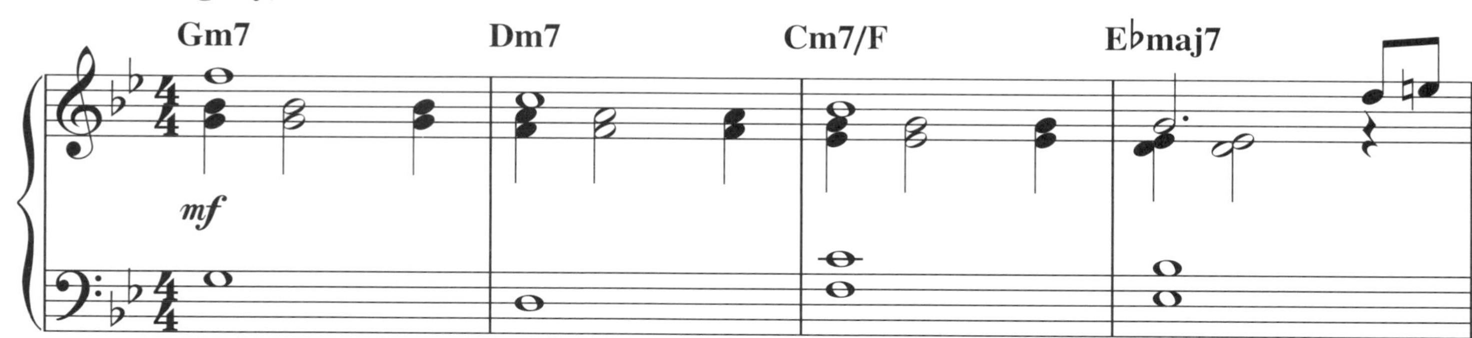

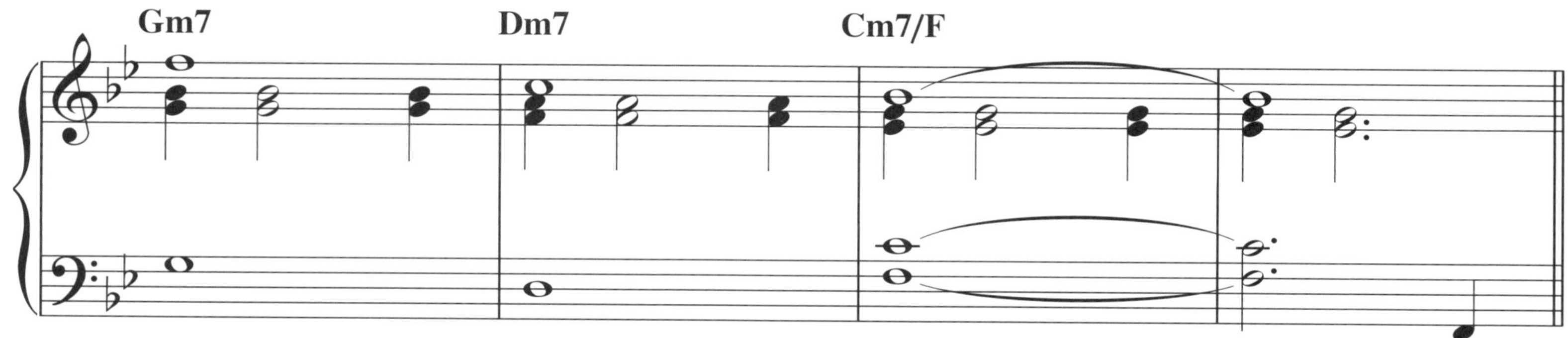

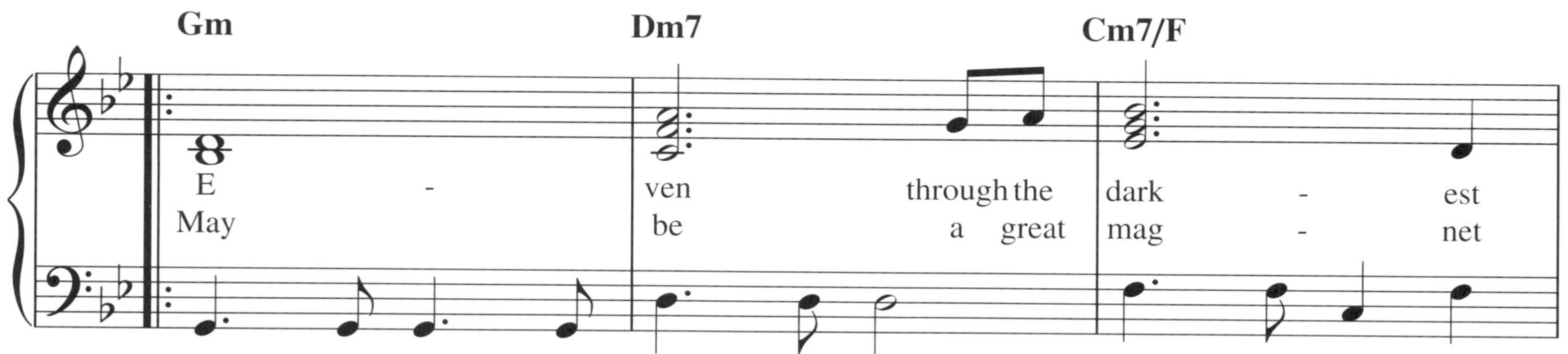

Cm7/F
Gm
thin,
truth,
al -
Or may -

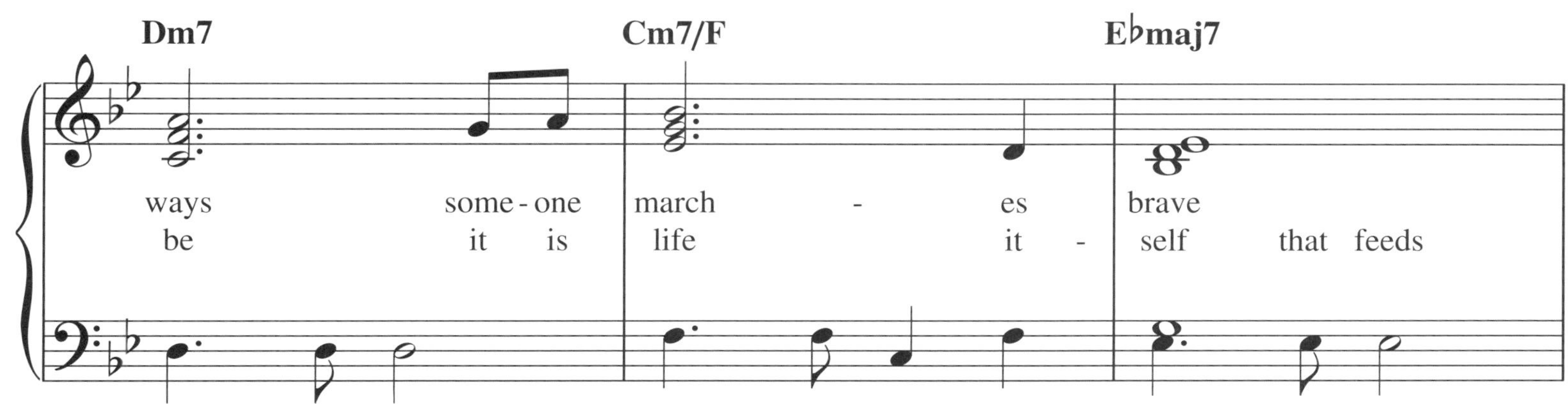
Dm7
Cm7/F
E♭maj7
ways some - one march - es brave
be it is life it - self that feeds

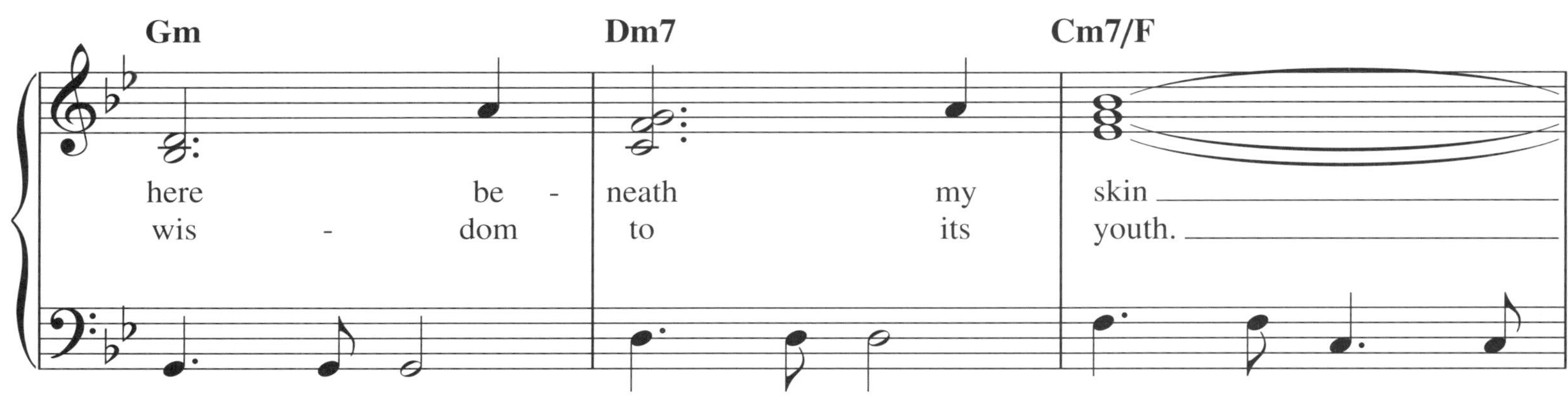
Gm
Dm7
Cm7/F
here be - neath my skin
wis - dom to its youth.

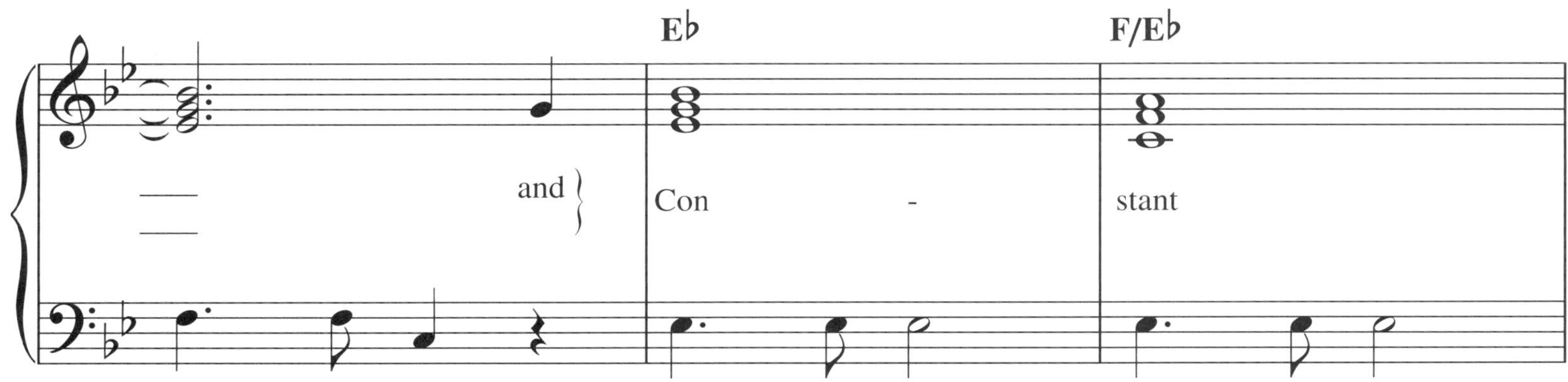
E♭
F/E♭
and
Con - stant

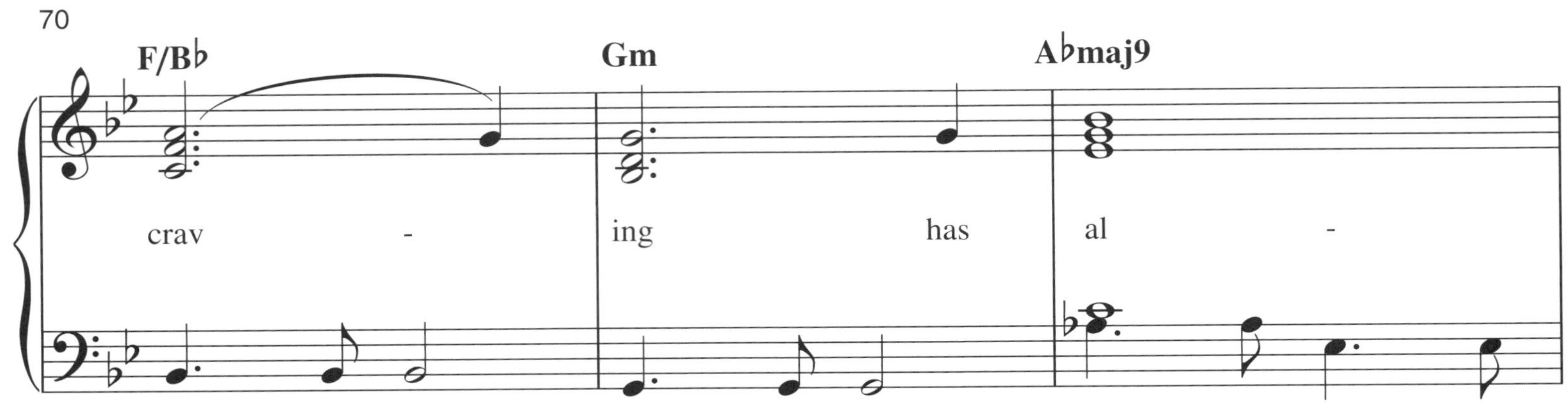
F/B♭
Gm
A♭maj9
crav - ing has al -

A♭
Gm
ways been.

E♭
F/E♭
F/B♭
Gm
Con - stant crav - ing has

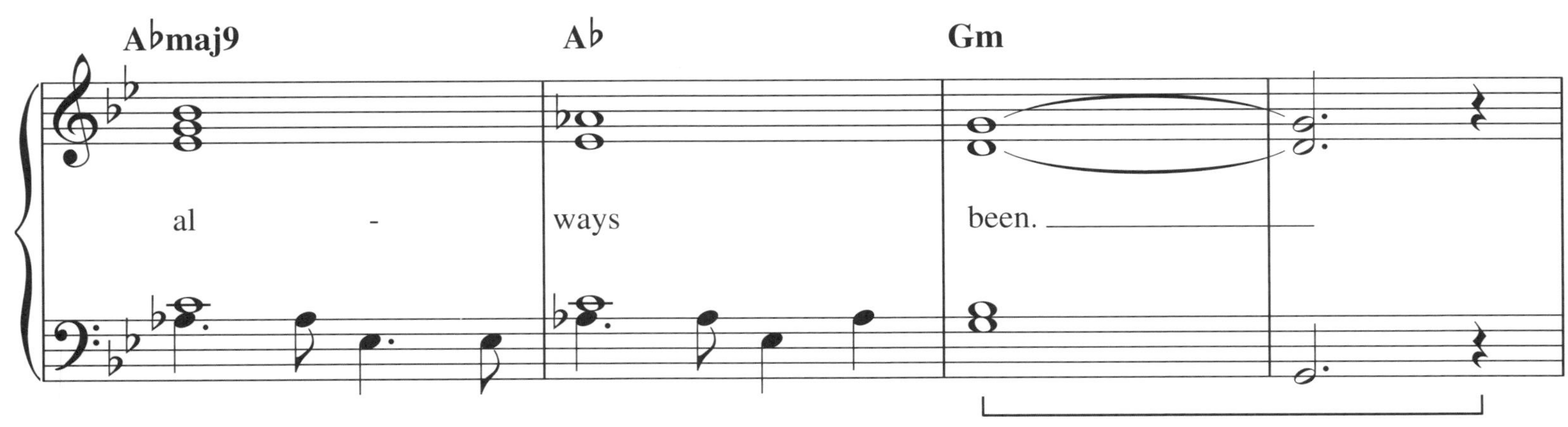
A♭maj9
A♭
Gm
al - ways been.

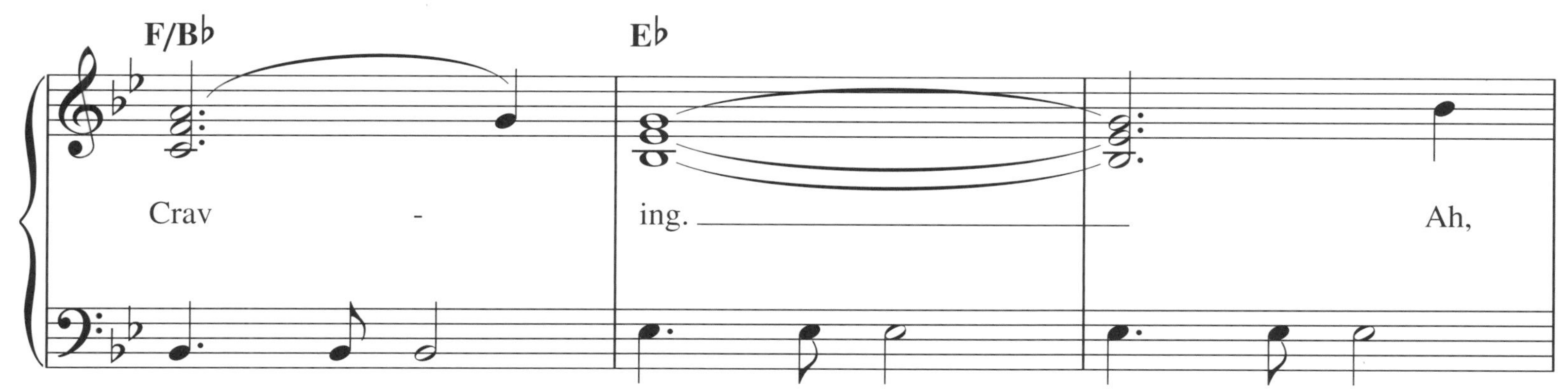
F/B♭
E♭
Crav - ing. Ah,

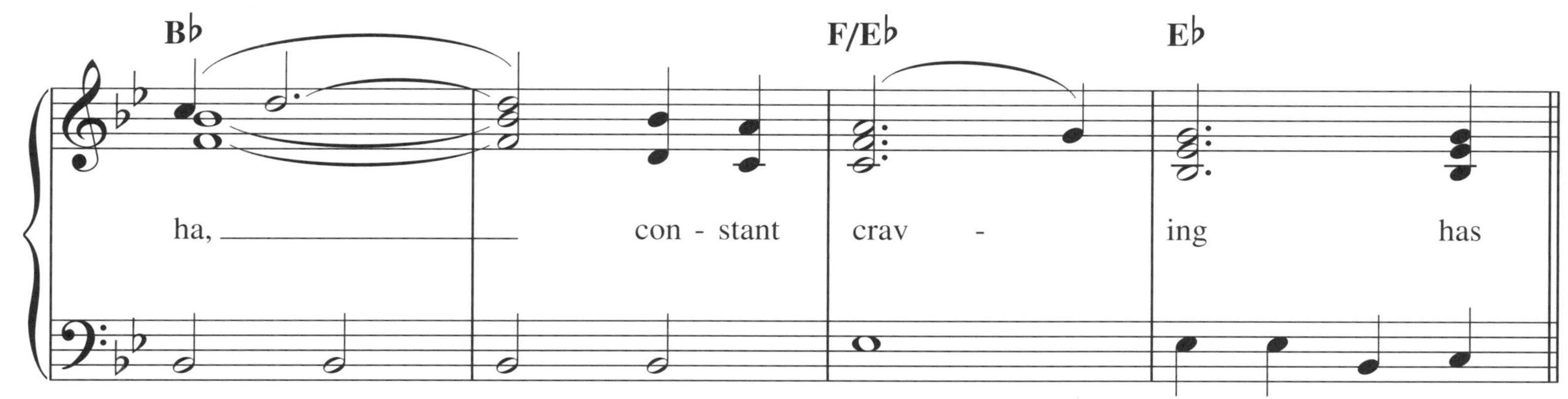
B♭
F/E♭
E♭
ha, con - stant crav - ing has

F
E♭
al - ways been.

Repeat ad lib.
F
E♭
Has al - ways been.
rit.

MAN IN THE MIRROR

Words and Music by GLEN BALLARD
and SIEDAH GARRETT

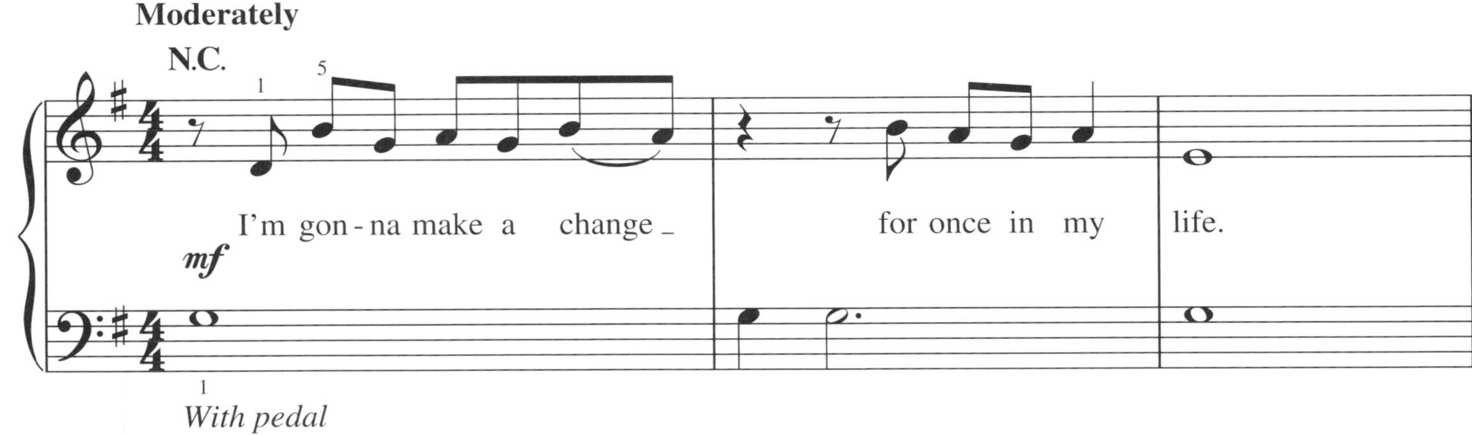

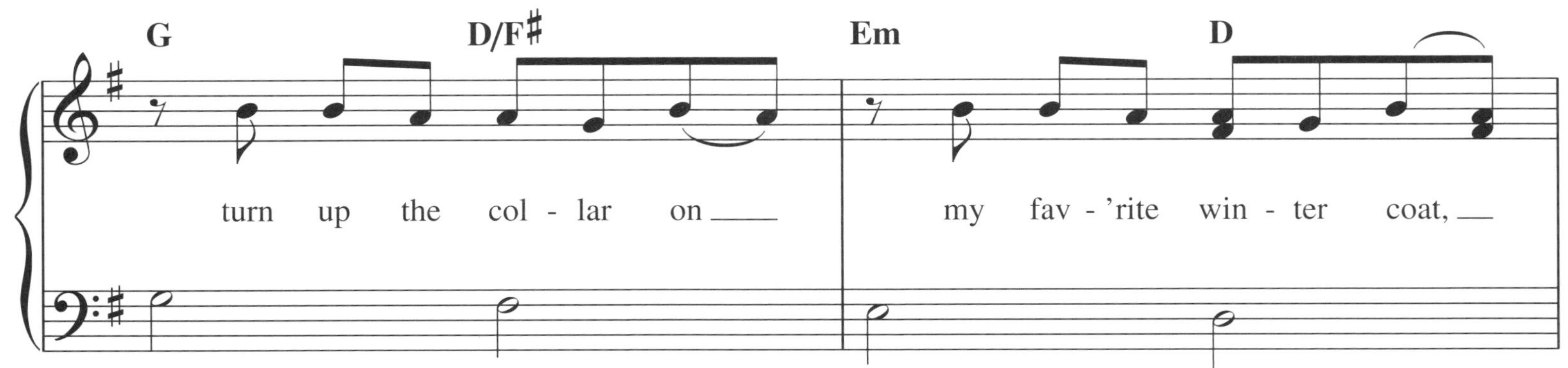

Cmaj7
this wind is blow - in' my mind. I see the kids

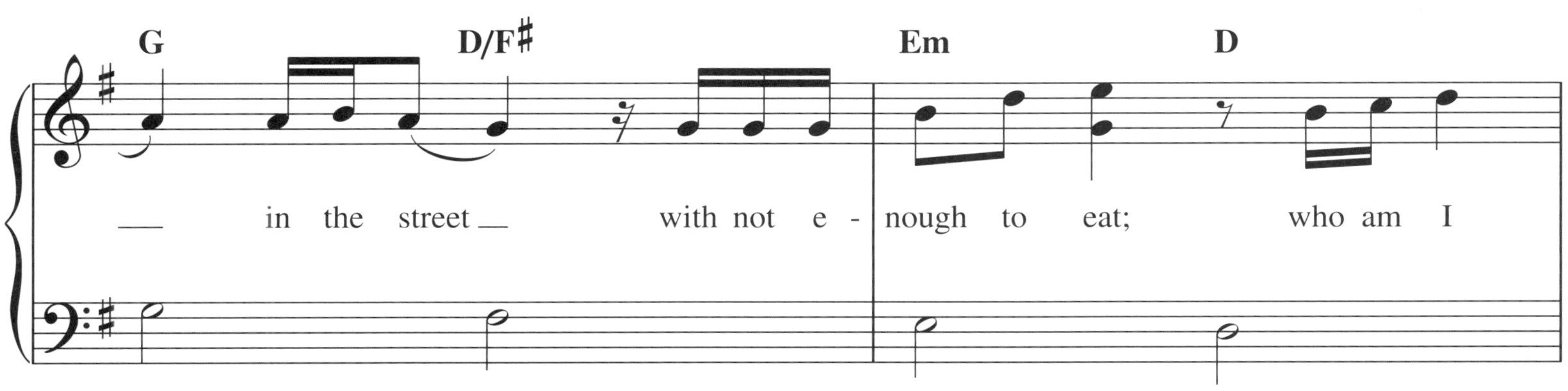
G D/F♯ Em D
in the street with not e - nough to eat; who am I

Cmaj7
to be blind, pre - tend - ing not to see their needs?

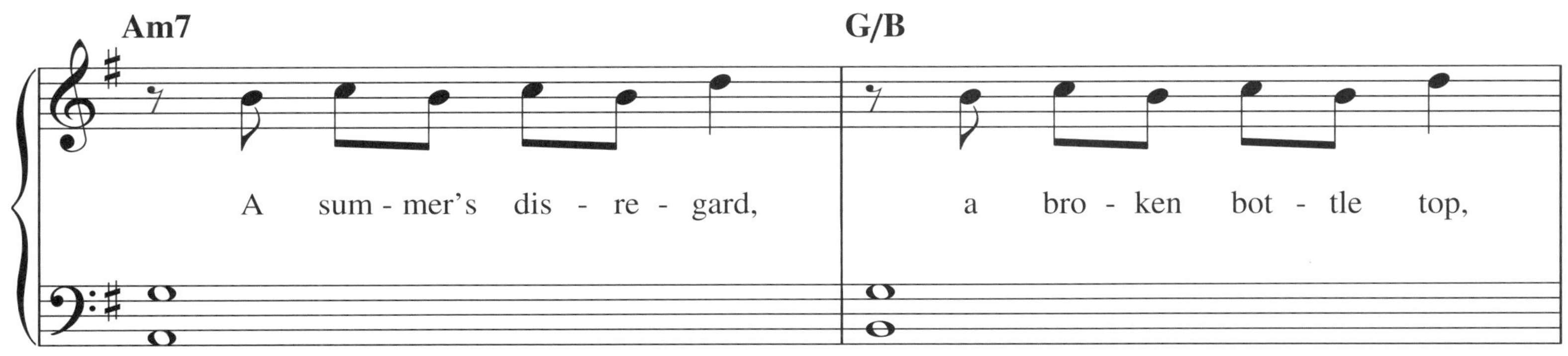
Am7 G/B
A sum - mer's dis - re - gard, a bro - ken bot - tle top,

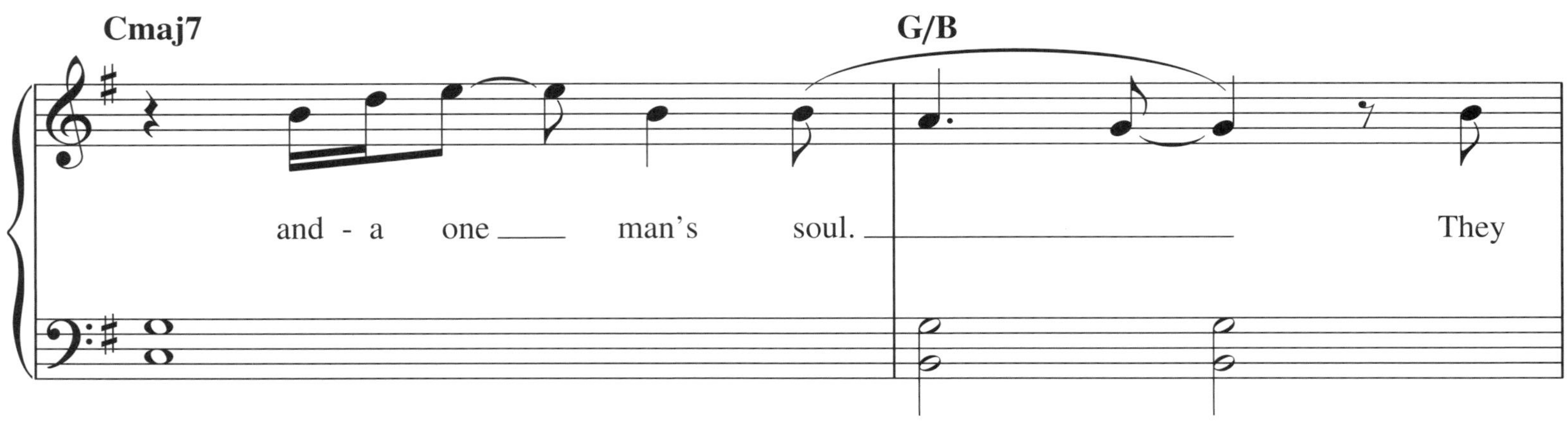
Cmaj7
G/B
and - a one man's soul.
They

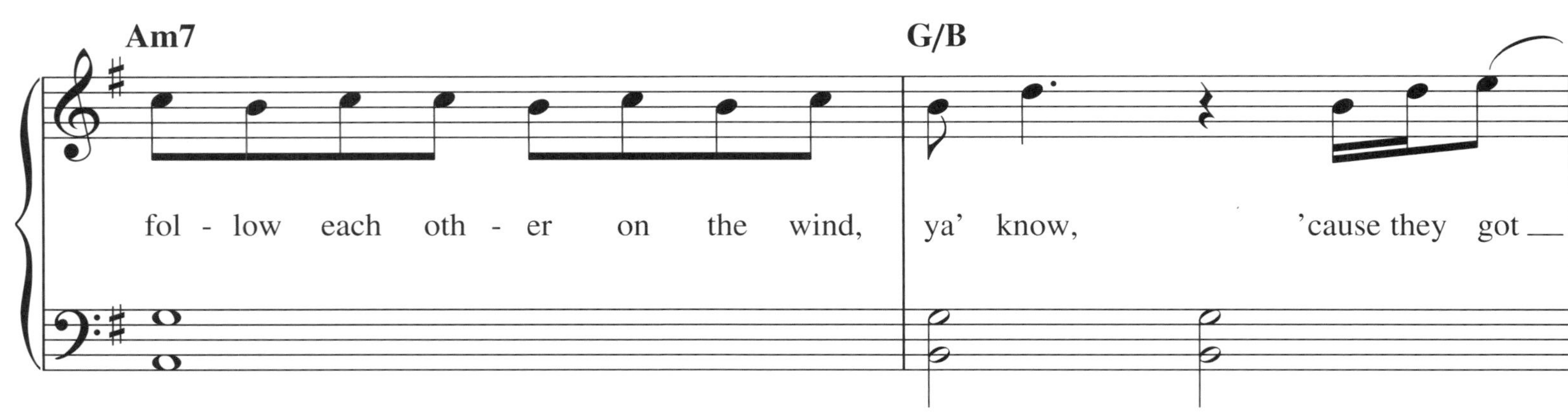
Am7
G/B
fol - low each oth - er on the wind,
ya' know,
'cause they got

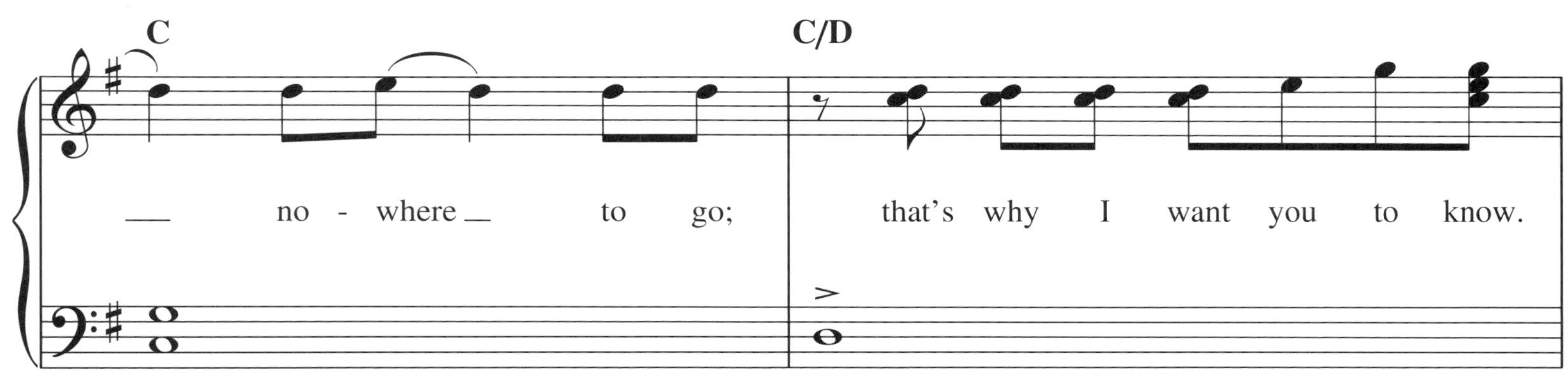
C
C/D
no - where to go;
that's why I want you to know.

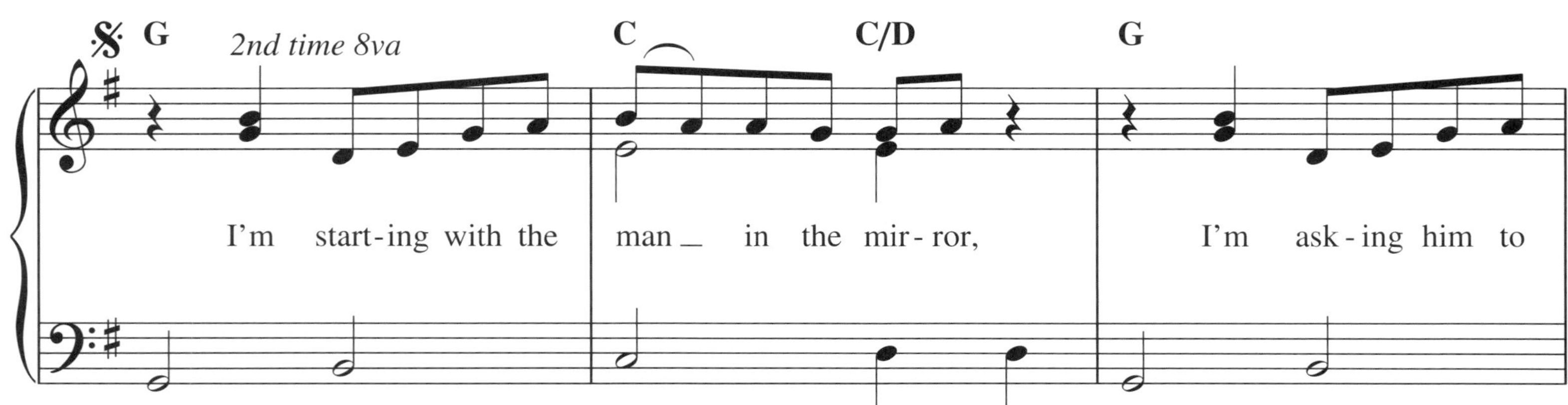
G
2nd time 8va
C
C/D
G
I'm start-ing with the
man in the mir-ror,
I'm ask-ing him to

C
C/D
G
change his ways.
And no mes - sage could have

C
A/C♯
D7♯9
been an - y clear-er: If you
wan-na make the world a bet - ter place, take a

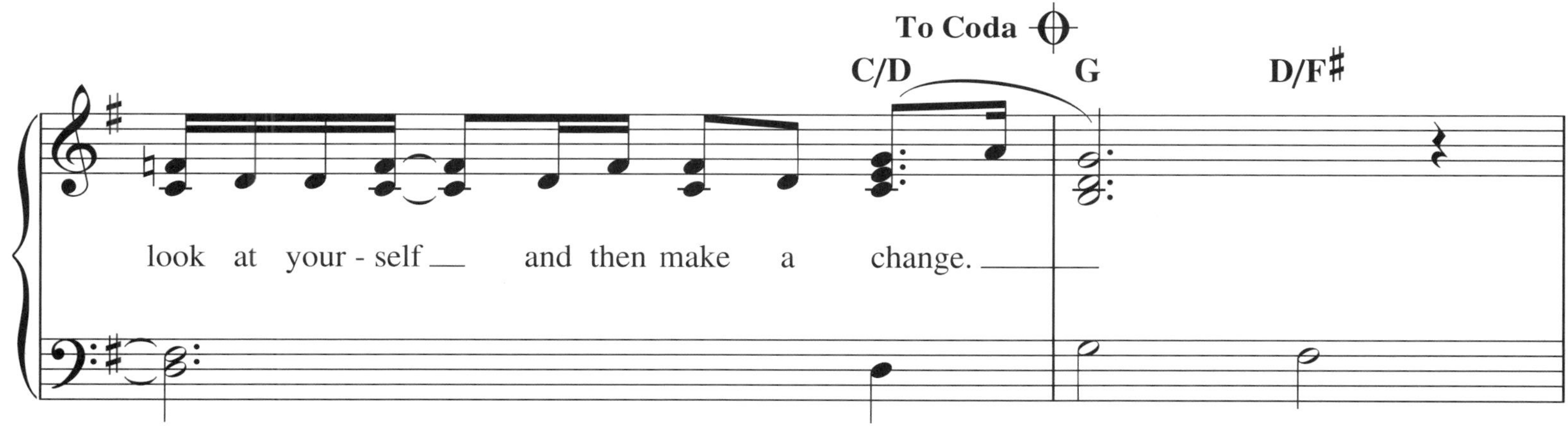
To Coda
C/D
G
D/F♯
look at your - self and then make a change.

Em
D
C
D
Na na na na na na na
na na nah.

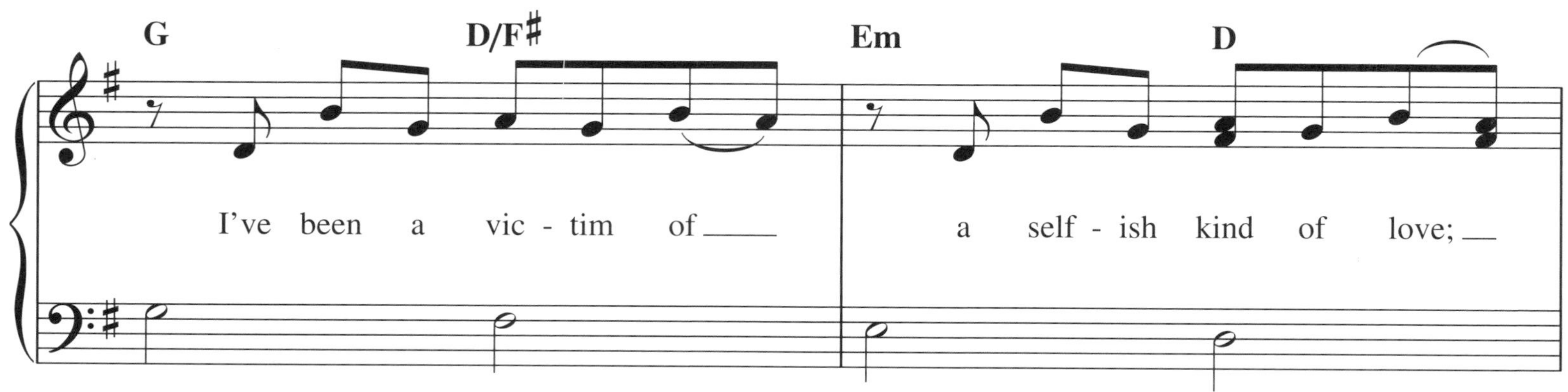
G
D/F♯
Em
D
I've been a vic - tim of ___
a self - ish kind of love; ___

C
G
D/F♯
it's time that I re - al - ize ___
that there are
some with no home, _ not a

Em
D
Cmaj7
nick - el to loan; could it be
real - ly me pre - tend - ing that they're

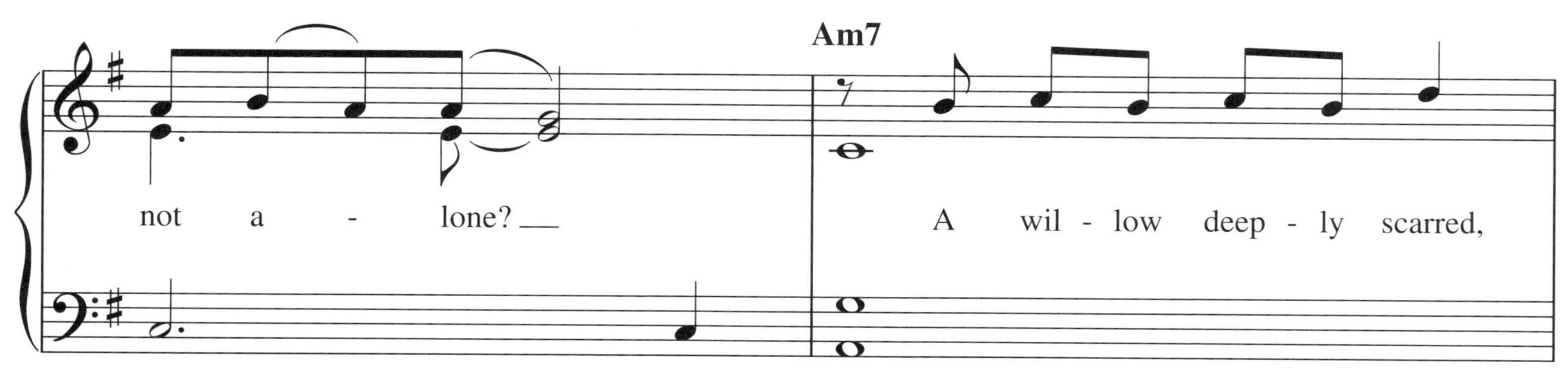
Am7
not a - lone? ___
A wil - low deep - ly scarred,

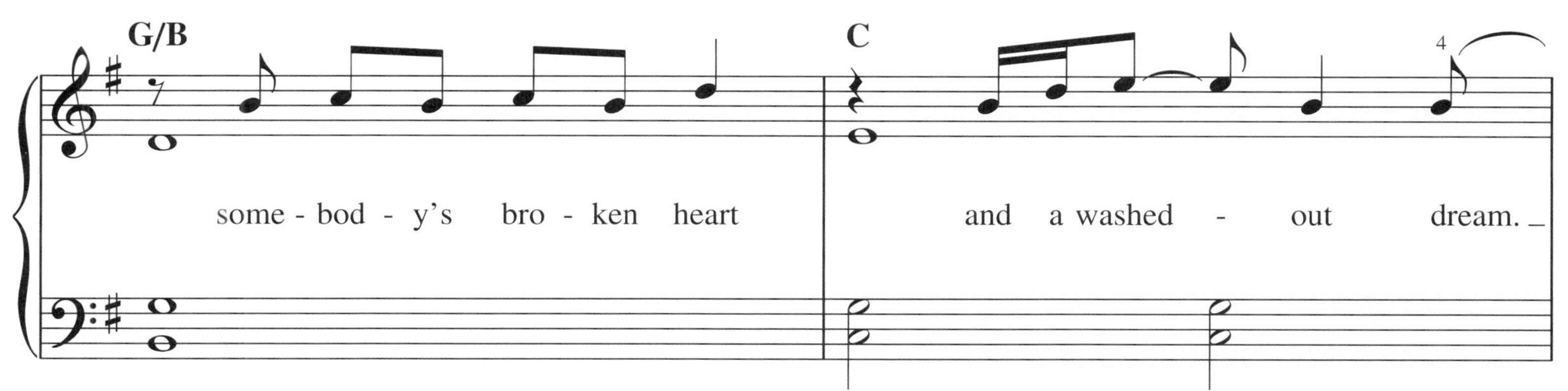
G/B
C
4
some - bod - y's bro - ken heart
and a washed - out dream.

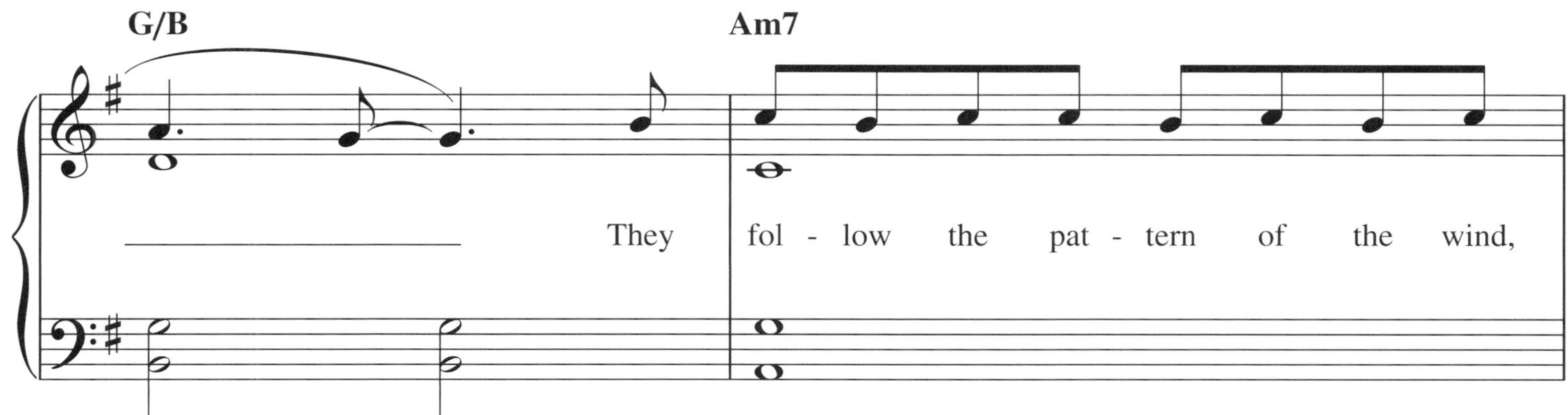
G/B
Am7
They
fol - low the pat - tern of the wind,

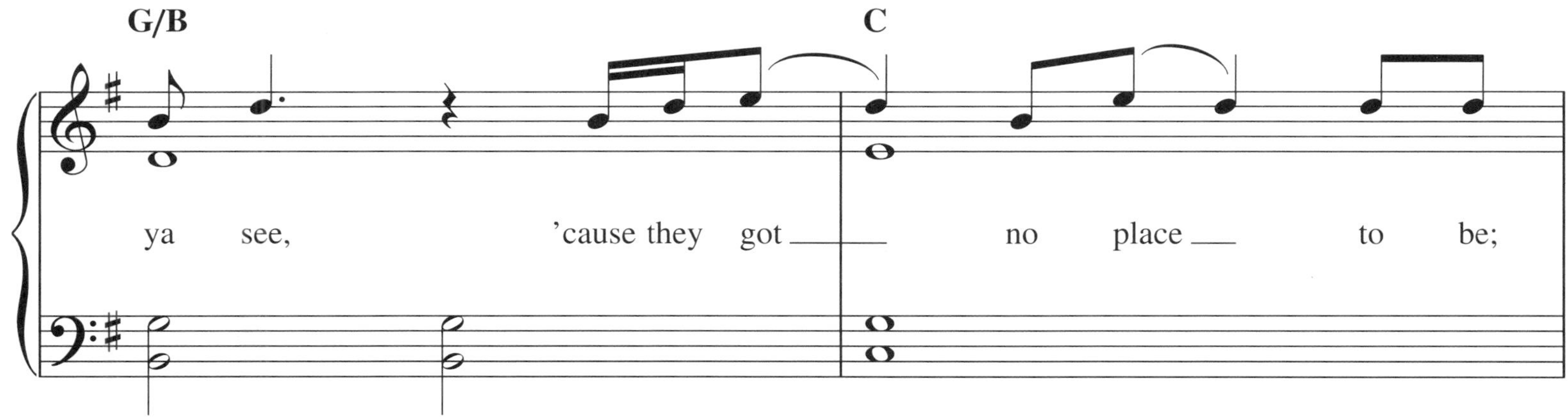
G/B
C
ya see, 'cause they got
no place to be;

C/D
D.S. al Coda
that's why I'm start - ing with me.

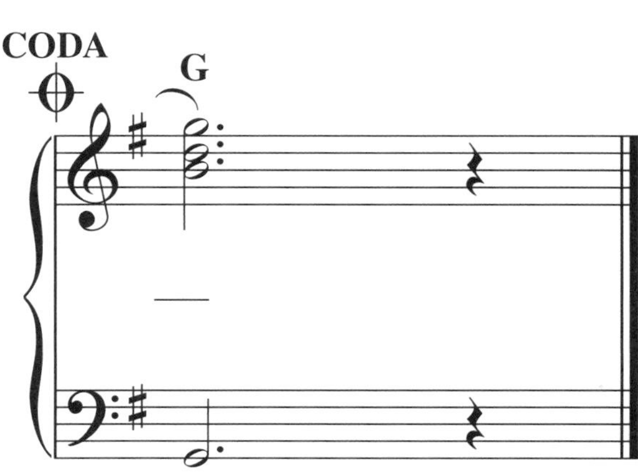
CODA
G

CONTROL

Words and Music by JAMES HARRIS III
and TERRY LEWIS

trol. ___ Nev - er gon - na stop. Con - trol. ___ To
trol. ___ Now I've got a lot. Con - trol. ___ To

get what I want. Con - trol. ___ I got to have a lot. ___ Con -
get what I want. Con - trol. ___ I'm nev - er gon - na stop. _ Con -

1.
Dm7
trol. ___ And now I'm all grown up.
trol. ___ And now I'm all grown up.

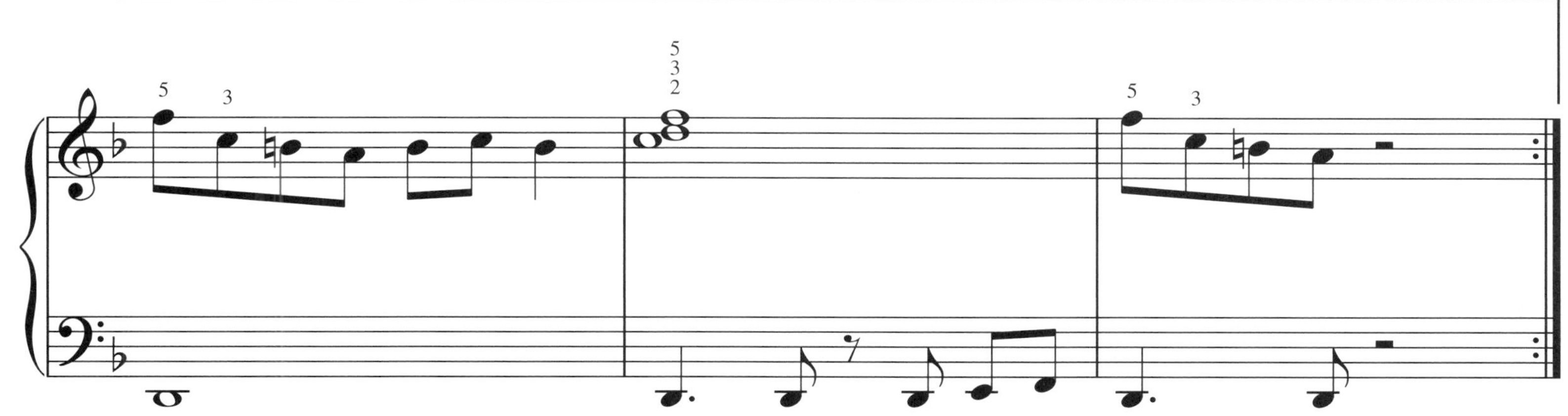

2.
Jam,
woo, woo.
Reb - el,

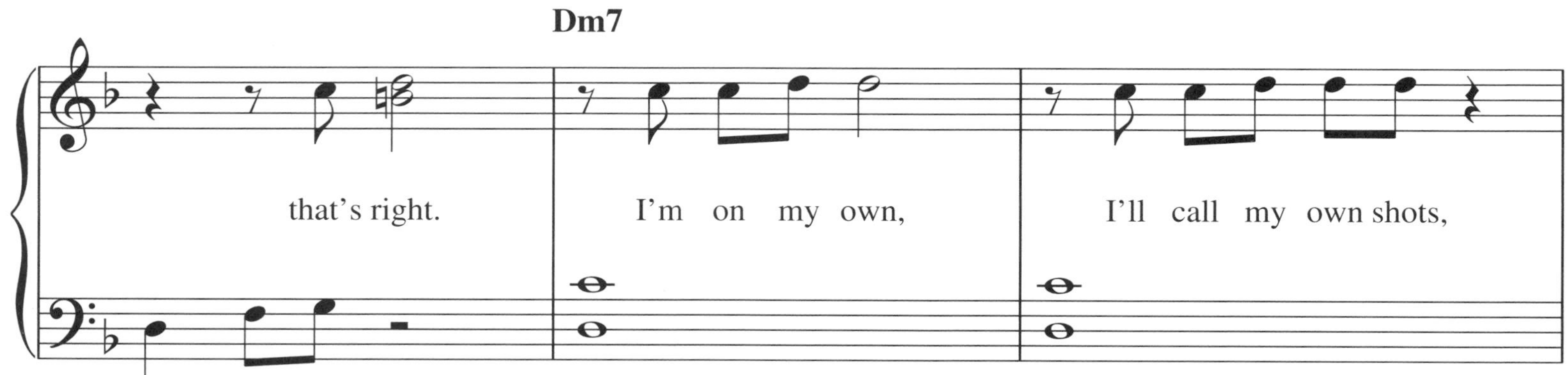
Dm7
that's right.
I'm on my own,
I'll call my own shots,

B♭
thank you.
Got my own mind,

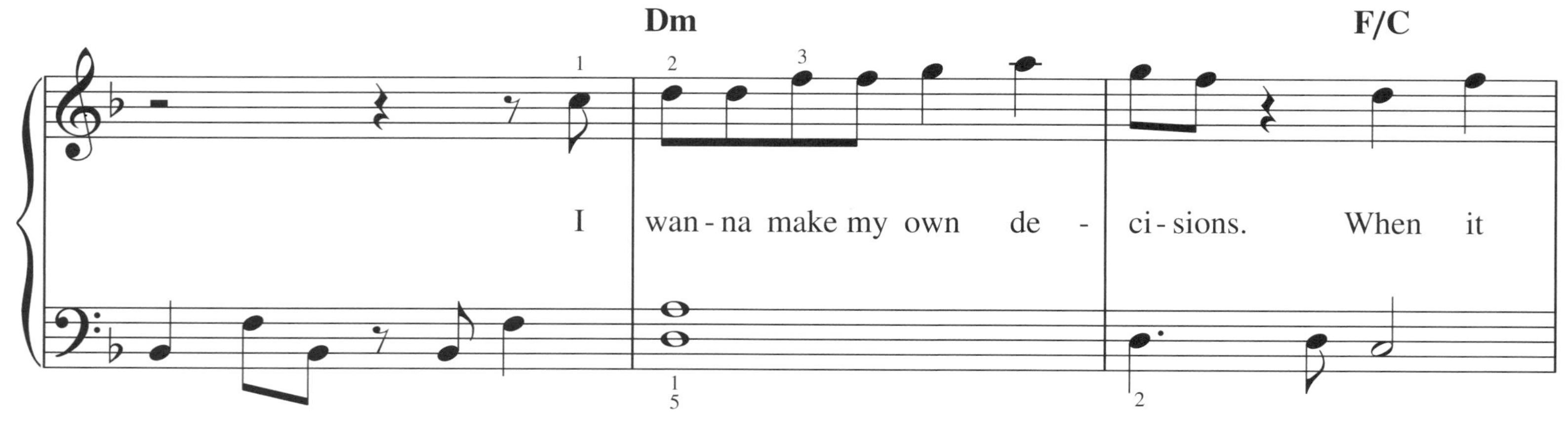
Dm
F/C
I wan - na make my own de - ci - sions. When it

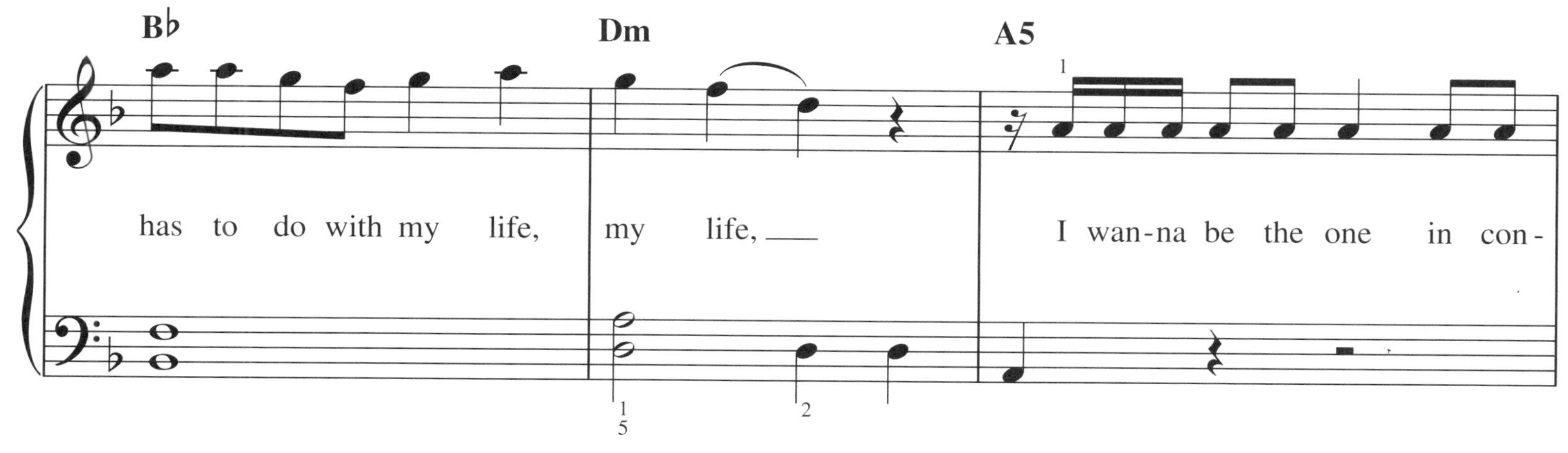
B♭
Dm
A5
has to do with my life,
my life,
I wan-na be the one in con-

Dm
trol.
So
let me take you by the hand and

lead you on this dance.
'Cause what I got, it's be-
cause I took a chance.

I don't wan - na rule the world, just
wan - na run my life.
So

5
make your life a lit - tle eas - i - er,
when you get the chance, just take con -
1
5

2
5
2
trol. ___
Now I've got a lot, oo. Con -
trol. ___ To
5

3
2
3
get what I want, con -
trol. ___ I'm
nev - er gon - na stop. Con -

A5
Dm
5
trol. ___
Now I'm all grown up, woo!
Free ______

at last.
I'm
out here on my own.

Oo, oo, oo,
yeah.
Hee!
Now control this.

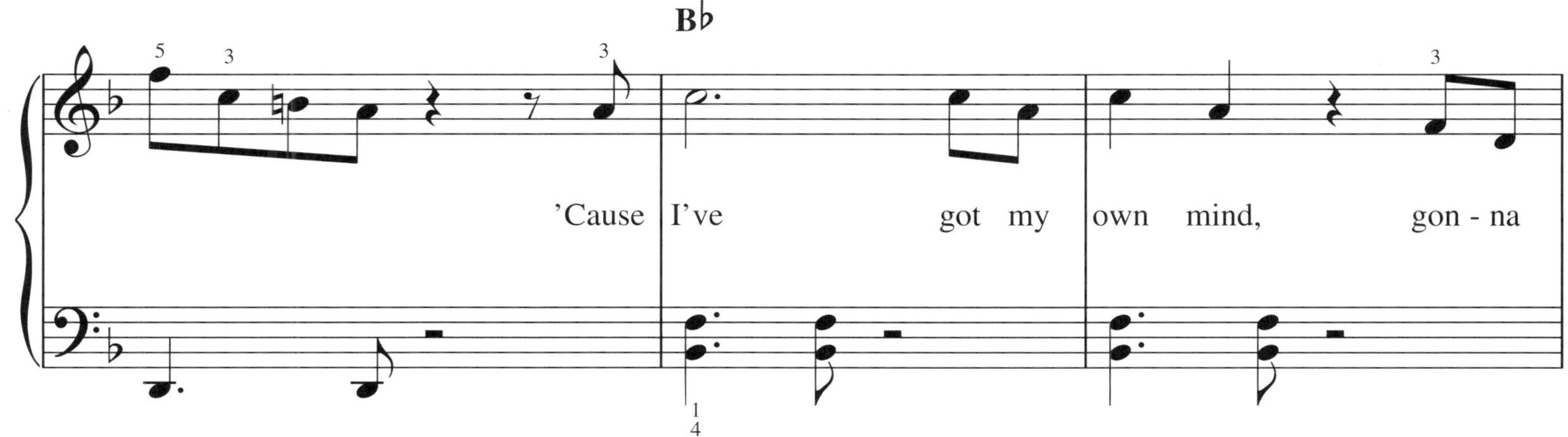
B♭
'Cause
I've got my
own mind, gon - na

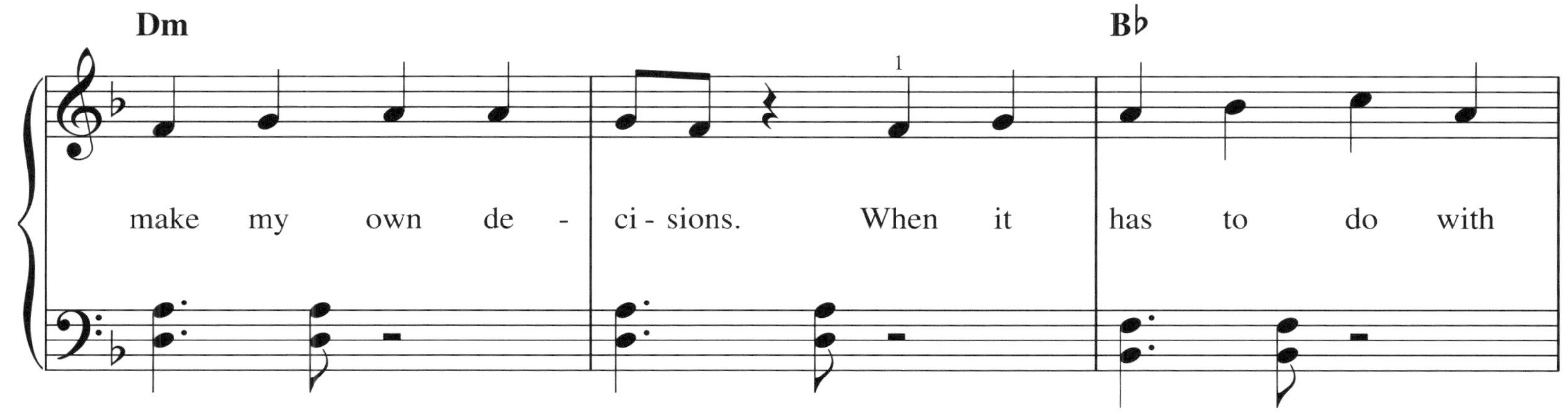
Dm
B♭
make my own de -
ci - sions. When it
has to do with

A5
my life,
I wan - na be the one in con -

Dm
trol.
I'm in con - trol, uh.

I'm in con - trol, uh.
I'm

in con - trol, uh.
I'm in con - trol, uh.

glee-full collections!

Get hip with music featured on the blockbuster TV show.

Ukulele

Glee
00701722 Ukulele $14.99

Manuscript Paper

Glee
00210119 .... $3.50

Piano/Vocal/Guitar

Glee
00313479 P/V/G $16.99

More Songs from Glee
00313491 P/V/G $16.99

Glee – The Christmas Album
00313566 P/V/G $16.99

Glee – The Showstoppers
00313512 P/V/G $16.99

Glee – Journey to Regionals
00313516 P/V/G $12.99

Glee – The Power of Madonna
00313507 P/V/G $14.99

Glee – The Rocky Horror Glee Show
00313528 P/V/G $12.99

Glee – The Warblers
00313567 P/V/G $16.99

Glee – Season Two, Volume 4
00313533 P/V/G $16.99

Glee – Season Two, Volume 5
00313540 P/V/G $16.99

Glee – Season Two, Volume 6
00313582 P/V/G $16.99

Glee – Season Three, Volume 7
00313634 P/V/G $16.99

Glee – Piano Play-Along Vol. 102
00312043 P/V/G $15.99

Glee – The 3D Concert Movie Motion Picture Soundtrack
00313614 P/V/G $17.99

Piano

Glee
00316140 Easy Piano $14.99
00316148 Big-Note Piano $14.99
00316147 Five-Finger Piano $8.99

More Songs from Glee
00316150 Easy Piano $14.99

Glee – Easy Piano CD Play-Along Vol. 30
00312194 Book/CD Pack $14.99

Glee – The Christmas Album
00316162 Easy Piano $14.99

Glee – The Power of Madonna
00316142 Easy Piano $12.99

Glee – The Showstoppers
00316145 Easy Piano $14.99

Glee – Popular Songs Series
arr. Jennifer Linn
00296834 .... $10.99

Glee – Piano Chord Songbook
00312270 Lyrics/Chord Symbols/Piano Chord Diagrams $12.99

Glee – Piano Duet Play-Along Vol. 42
00290590 Book/CD Pack $16.99

Glee – The Warblers
00316169 Easy Piano $14.99

Glee – Season Two, Volume 4
00316158 Easy Piano $14.99

Glee – Season Two, Volume 5
00316159 Easy Piano $14.99

Glee – Season Two, Volume 6
00316173 Easy Piano $14.99

Glee – Season Three, Volume 7
00316186 Easy Piano $14.99

Guitar

Glee INCLUDES TAB
00702286 Easy Guitar – Notes & Tab ... $16.99

Glee Guitar Collection INCLUDES TAB
00691050 Guitar Recorded Versions ... $19.99

Vocal

Glee – The Singer's Series
00230061 Women's Edition Vol. 1 .... $14.99
00230062 Women's Edition Vol. 2 .... $14.99
00230063 Women's Edition Vol. 3 .... $14.99
00230064 Men's Edition Vols. 1-3 .... $16.99
00230065 Duets Edition Vols. 1-3 .... $16.99

Glee – Pro Vocal Book/CD Packs
00740437 Male/Female Edition Vol. 8 ... $16.99
00740440 Male/Female Edition Vol. 9 ... $21.99
00740443 Male/Female Edition Vol. 10 ... $15.99

Glee – Sing with the Choir Book/CD Pack
00333059 SATB, Vol. 14 .... $16.99
00333377 SATB, Vol. 17 .... $17.99

Glee Vocal Method & Songbook
00312081 Book/CD Pack $14.99

Electronic Keyboard

Glee – E-Z Play Today Vol. 88
00100287 .... $9.99

For More Information, See Your Local Music Dealer, Or Write To:

7777 W. Bluemound Rd. P.O. Box 13819 Milwaukee, WI 53213

Prices, contents and availability subject to change without notice.

www.halleonard.com

0312